The Wreckhouse

By

Christopher Butt

The Wreckhouse

Copyright © 2026 by Christopher Butt

Front cover illustration © by DarkWinter Designs

First Printing: January 2026

Published by **DarkWinter Press**: www.darkwinterlit.com

ISBN: 978-1-998441-38-9

Also by Christopher Butt at DarkWinter Press:

In the Lair of the Kraken

Praise for *In the Lair of the Kraken*

"Butt's prose is often straight-forward, but his images are vivid.
I flew through the collection."

Alison Manley, Miramichi Reader

This book is dedicated to my partner in crime at St. John Ambulance, Victor Kostiff. He shared my offbeat humour, love of Science Fiction, and was an excellent First Aid Instructor. My friend, you left us way too soon.

Table of Contents

Foreword

Well, folks, here it is, the classic sports cliché: Can the rookie surpass his first season, or in this case, his first book? Well dear reader, that's up to you.

My first book, *In the Lair of the Kraken,* was a dream come true. However, after the thrill of getting my first book published, the horror set in. I must keep writing, and what the heck is going to happen in the next one? Cue the sweating author staring at an empty laptop screen.

While my first collection was stories that I had written over the past few years, the stories for this collection were written directly for it. Between the covers are stories about the town of Otherville, my fictional town in Ontario, an immortal hunter named Hugo Macdaniel, and other 'one offs' that may lead to something down the road.

Included as well are six stories taking place in, or partially in, my home province of Newfoundland and Labrador. And because it's me, there's also a story inspired by a Rush song, which in turn was inspired by a poem by Samuel Taylor Coleridge. Got to love Neil Peart. A story inspired by a friend's dream and a Niagara-on-the-Lake style town round out the bunch.

In the end, it was both hard work and a joy to put these stories together. Some flowed, while others were paused halfway, due to either running out of steam or wicked writer's block. It was also satisfying to put down several ideas that had been with me for years. It was good to get them out of my head to make room for other tenants. I just wish they paid rent.

Finally, I want to thank you, one and all, for having this book in your hands, whether by purchasing it or borrowing it from the library. Supporting Canadian authors is crucial to keeping our stories, be it fiction or non, alive. Cheers to you all, and read safely.

"The blizzards near the Wreckhouse make it feel like you're living in a flour sack."

—Local saying in Newfoundland

Billy Thompson and the Old Hag

Heart's Content, Newfoundland and Labrador

Little Billy Thompson was running for his life. He already had cuts on his face from the rocks that were thrown at him, and scrapes on his knees where he had fallen. As he ran around the back of the school, Billy found the caretaker's shed. He tried the door, but it was locked.

"Billy Thompson, you little frigger!" Tucker Wallace yelled, as he and his three cronies ran around the school. "We're going to kill ya!"

Billy ran to the side of the shed and spotted a long piece of sheet metal. He scrambled behind it and knelt. He put his hand over his mouth to disguise his breathing, but instead tasted blood on his fingers. He gasped when he heard Tucker try the shed door.

"I know you're here, Billy," Tucker taunted. "You can't hide from us. We're like those dogs that find drugs in the airport. I can smell your fear or, what is that? Did you wet yourself, Billy?"

Billy held his breath and closed his eyes. He could hear the bullies laughing and calling him names. Tears formed, but he quickly wiped them away and opened one of his eyes tentatively. He saw one of bullies staring at him through the small space between the wall and the metal sheet.

"There he is!" the boy shouted.

Billy started to cry as the bullies shook the sheet. Suddenly the metal pressed against him, and he was forced into the side of the shed. He could hear the bullies laughing. As the metal closed in, Billy started to labour in his breathing. Soon, he couldn't get any air at all. He gazed up at the small opening at the top of the metal sheet.

"Please," he cried.

Billy stared up at the small patch of sky. As his breath disappeared, the opening morphed into the skylight over his bed. The old memory faded, but the pressure didn't. Billy found himself pinned to his bed, unable to move. On top of that, his bladder was painfully reminding him of the three beers he'd had after supper.

"Please," he whispered, using any air he could get to form the word. He closed his eyes and forced himself to be calm. He remembered that Star Wars movie, *Rogue One*. One of the characters had a mantra that he chanted:

"I am one with the force and the force is with me,"

Billy repeated the line several times, but to no avail. His Aunt Sarah had described this situation to Billy years ago. She called it the 'Old Hag'.

"I tell you Billy, I couldn't move to save my life. When I realized she wouldn't take me, she left, but I tell you it was some scary."

Billy remembered Sarah fondly. She'd looked after him when he got home from school while his parents worked. Gave him peppermint knob candies and peanut butter toast. She also gave him advice on bullies.

"Turning the other cheek will only get you so far. Eventually you have stand up to them, or they will own you for life."

When she died, not only did it leave a huge hole in his heart, but in the whole town. Everyone loved Sarah and her kind spirit. Hers was one of the biggest funerals in the small community. The following week at school, he took her advice. He was suspended for a week by the principal, and grounded for a month by his parents, but Tucker never bothered him again.

That is, until now. Billy could see Tucker's face in his mind, laughing.

"Ah, Billy Thompson's got the old hag."

"Fuck off!" Billy shouted, and Tucker's face faded away. Squeezing his eyes, Billy concentrated on his breathing. It was shallow and his lungs hurt. His bladder also reared its ugly head with a less-than-gentle reminder.

In his mind, he found himself on stage in a small theatre. He was tied tightly to a chair, and he couldn't breathe. His bladder was full and begging for a release. The theatre was full of people he knew. Friends he grew up with, his co-workers at the Employment Centre, his parents, siblings, and his Aunt Sarah. In the front row was his ex-wife Carly and her arsehole husband Jock. They were all sitting quietly.

Billy could feel the daggers they threw at him with their eyes. They were judging him.

He opened his eyes and spotted the old CD player on his night table. He smiled as music came into his mind. Pink Floyd, Rush, and Iron Maiden appeared on stage, filling his thoughts with the good times of the eighties. Even Taylor Swift, a favourite of his niece, appeared next to David Gilmour and Alex Lifeson riffing on their guitars.

"Trouble. Trouble. Trouble."

"Yes, Taylor, I know I'm in trouble," Billy said, shaking his head. He let the quasi-retro/new music concert play in his head until Freddy Mercury and David Bowie showed up, his subconscious deciding to have a little fun with him.

"Do, do, do, da, da, do, do. Under pressure."

Billy closed his eyes and forced Queen and the Thin White Duke off the stage. He conjured up the Floyd again to play 'Wish You Were Here' in its entirety. Richard Wright's synthesizers brought a calmness to Billy's current state.

As Floyd's tribute to their former front man floated in his mind, Billy turned his head and spotted the picture his ex-wife on the bureau. It was of the two of them, cross country skiing at Marble Mountain outside of Corner Brook.

Carly, a born athlete, could do anything. Even though Billy could hold his own, Carly was head and shoulders above anything he could do. A five-foot-eight, fit woman rocking a shock of blond hair, Billy was in love the first time he laid eyes on her.

They met at a university track meet and became acquaintances, meeting up again at other sporting events over the years. After graduation, Billy ran into her again at a job interview. As they waited their turns, they talked about the old days, and as she was called in, he asked her out. She accepted.

A year later, they were married and living the dream. After two years, however, it became a nightmare. After trying to have a baby, they went to a doctor who informed them that Billy had a low sperm count. They talked about adopting, but it went nowhere.

Soon rumours swirled around the marriage. Confrontations, accusations, confirmations of betrayal, a letter of notice of divorce, and it was all over. Carly married one of her old beaus from high school, Jock McDavid, hockey star on the rise. She was soon pregnant and living the life of a successful hockey wife.

"Bitch," Billy thought. Suddenly Carly and Tucker replaced Floyd on the stage. They were pointing and laughing at him.

"What's the matter, Billy?" Tucker asked. "Can't get it up? Oh yeah, you don't have any shells for your artillery piece."

"He was a lousy lover anyway," Carly sneered. "Jock, now *that* man is a real lover. Do you know what they called him in school? Jock the Cock, and he had a real gun."

Tucker and Carly laughed again. Tears rolled down Billy's face. He turned back to the picture and vowed to throw it out. A thought occurred to him that it would be better to send it anonymously to Jock with a letter saying what a great time Carly was. Leave it suggestive.

In his mind, Carly and Tucker were kissing. They turned and sneered at him.

"Stop!" Billy shouted, and the couple disappeared. He panicked and tried to control his breathing again. It was rapid, and he was having trouble getting air into his lungs. As he tried to inhale, he felt himself losing control of his bladder. The pain was too much, and he could feel the piss coming.

"Jesus, I don't want to wet the bed!" He struggled some more but still couldn't move. He forced the mantra into his mind. Nothing was working. He tried to move again. As he struggled to free his arms, he lost control of his bladder.

"No!" he whispered as his bladder released. Billy could smell the urine as his underwear and pajama pants became soaked. The bedclothes and mattress became sticky, as his bladder finally emptied.

Despite pissing himself and being uncomfortable, Billy felt a wave of relief come over him. The release of pressure calmed him down a little. His head fell back on his pillow, and he was able to concentrate. However, not for long.

"Oh, what's this? Little Billy Thompson peed himself." Tucker's face entered his mind. The boy was laughing. "Just like you did in grade school. Little Willy Billy pissed himself."

Tucker's laughter echoed his Billy's head. Angry, Billy shouted, "Go away Tucker. You're dead."

A confused look passed over Tucker's face.

"You died driving your transport truck through the Wreckhouse on a stormy night. The high winds blew you right off the road."

Tucker yelled at Billy. "No, I didn't!"

"Stupid Tucker the Trucker. Wouldn't listen to the warnings. Thought you were better than everyone else. Well, you were stupid, and you died."

"Well, you got the hag and pissed your bed."

"Better than being dead."

Tucker looked confused. Billy smiled as Tucker faded away. No longer able to live rent-free in Billy's head.

"See ya, you little frigger."

Billy closed his eyes again. Even though the pressure was off, he still couldn't move, and the stench of urine filled his nose.

"What am I going to do?" he thought. He closed his eyes, and the stage reappeared. Carly was gone, only to be replaced by his mother, who was shaking her head.

"Your father would be some ashamed of you. Pissing the bed at your age."

"I got the hag, Ma, what do you want me to do? I can hardly breath and can't move."

"Whose fault is that now?" his mother asked.

"I don't know!" Billy screamed at his mother. "Maybe instead of criticizing me, you could help."

His mother shot Billy a hateful looked and turned away. She disappeared off the stage. Billy put his head down and sighed. The ticking of the clock on his bed drummed away. When he opened his eyes, he saw the reason for his lack of breath.

A naked old crone sat on his chest. Her long nose leaned forward and touched his. He could smell her rotten breath, and tried to avoid her piercing red eyes.

"Billy Thompson. Billy Thompson," the crone said. "To get rid of me, you must curse someone else. Who will it be?"

"No. I won't curse anyone else. I can't!"

"Very well," the crone said, and put her hands over his eyes.

Billy found himself back on the stage. He was in a glass case that was filling with water. He pounded on the glass and screamed for help. Everyone in the audience clapped and cheered. Carly, Tucker, and his mother were in the front row.

As the water filled the case, Billy took one last breath and stared out at the audience. He didn't feel hate but pity.

"I can't curse anyone!" he yelled. "I can't." The water filled the case. In his mind Billy thought, *I forgive all of you.*

As his air ran out, Billy sank to the bottom of the case. He passed out, smelling of urine.

The shrill of the alarm woke Billy the next morning, and he slammed it with his hand. As he rolled out of bed, he saw the mess he had made, and the night came back to him.

Two hours later he was showered, had cleaned up the room, and had thrown out the sheets and the mattress. He called his mother, decided not to send Carly's husband the picture with a note, and made an appointment to talk about his childhood with a counselor.

When he walked out into the crisp fall air, Billy got into his car and headed towards the mall to get a new mattress. As he pulled into the parking lot, he spotted one of the men who bullied him as a kid. For a moment he thought about what the hag had said, and he was tempted. In the end, he just pointed at the man and smiled.

"You don't know how lucky you are."

Staged

Stephen Miller swerved the stolen car to avoid a deer in the middle of the road. The car left the road and bulldozed its way through the bushes, crashing into a large oak and killing the engine. His chest exploded in pain as he pushed himself off the steering wheel. The bullet in his right arm joined in the pain parade.

"Christ, what a disaster."

Grunting, he opened his door and slid out of the car. He landed on his knees and vomited. Using his good arm, he lifted himself up and stumbled around the car. He retrieved the gun from the passenger side, along with the small amount of cash he managed to take. He put the gun in his back pocket and the cash in his front left. He stumbled through the bushes and fallen trees back out to the road. Turning towards the car, he was satisfied that it was safely hidden among the debris.

A low mist hung over the road in the evening cold, and Stephen figured he was still a couple of kilometres from the safe house. He cursed as the pain in his chest and arm reminded him of his current circumstances. Half an hour later, Stephen came up to a sign that stated, "North Otherville Cemetery Grounds." He smiled, remembering the sign.

Painted underneath the sign was the phrase, "Welcome to North Otherville. It's a quiet neighbourhood." Stephen smiled at the joke.

Fog swirled around the headstones as Stephen walked by the fence. Another sign indicated the Catholics to the right, the Protestants and the rest to the left. Stephen stopped and leaned against the Catholic gate to catch his breath. Despite the coolness of the evening, he was sweating, and started to wonder if he was going to make it out of this caper alive.

As he walked along the graveyard, a house appeared out of the darkness. Smiling, Stephen recognized the house he and the others had scouted earlier that week. It was empty and in the middle of nowhere. It was a perfect hiding place after the job, or if something went wrong, the meeting point.

In front of the house was a sign with "Otherville Realty" written across the top. It had a picture of a beautiful dark-haired woman smiling back at him, and the name Rhonda Walker written beneath it. Stephen paused for a second as he looked at the name. Something at the back of his mind nagged at him. He knew the name but couldn't place it. Eventually he shook the thoughts away and moved on towards the house.

As he stumbled up the front steps, he noticed the house looked different. When they'd scouted the place, it had looked like it had a lot of fire damage, but now it looked brand new. Stephen wondered if he was at the right house. He dragged his memory in front of his eyes and confirmed it. Rundown house by the graveyard.

He turned to the solid oak door and hoped his partner Tyler had picked the lock earlier. He closed his eyes and held his breath as his thumb depressed the latch. He heard a click, let out a breath, opened the door, and stepped inside.

The house was dark and offered no relief from the chilly evening air. He walked into the living room and threw himself into a chair, only to fall through and hit the floor.

Stunned, his body screaming in pain, Stephen looked at the chair and realized it was made of cardboard. He got to his knees and pushed against the side table. It was plastic with a faux wood stain.

"What the—" he started to say, when he heard a noise upstairs. Stephen struggled to his feet and hid behind the wall. He held his breath as someone carefully came down the stairs. A tall, dark-haired woman step out into the living room. As she stared at the broken chair, Stephen lunged out and grabbed the woman by the throat, forcing his hand under her chin, silencing her.

"Don't move or struggle," Stephen whispered. "I'm not going to hurt you if you behave. Nod if you understand."

The woman slowly nodded. As he pressed her up against the wall, he recognized her from the picture on the sign. She looked scared, and despite his pain, Stephen felt a little aroused.

"What the hell is with the furniture, Rhonda?"

He released his grip just enough to allow her to speak.

"I'm trying to sell the house," she said nervously. "I placed fake furniture in here so the prospective buyer can see how it looks furnished. It's called 'staging'."

Stephen glanced at the kitchen and noticed the fridge and stove were cardboard cutouts. He shook his head.

"You mean there's nothing real in this place?"

"Only the bathroom," Rhonda answered.

Stephen nodded and jerked his head towards the stairs. Slowly, Rhonda led the way to the second floor with Stephen's gun pointing at her back. At the top of the stairs, he pushed Rhonda into the bathroom. The old tub had a sliding shower door.

"Get in the tub," he ordered.

Rhonda stepped in the tub, and he slid the door shut behind her.

"What are you going to do with me?"

He ignored her and looked in the mirror. It was the first time he took stock of his situation. He didn't like the look of it.

Stephen's reflection was a ghostly white face sweating a river. His arm throbbed, and he was wearing some of his stomach contents on his face. He turned on the water, rinsing his face and mouth, and dried his face with his jacket sleeve. He picked up his gun and walked out of the bathroom into the adjacent bedroom to clear his head and think.

Stephen glanced out the window at the graveyard. The mist still hung over the headstones. The ghostly glow of the lone streetlight reminded him of those old black and white horror movies.

As he turned away from the window, Stephen swore he saw someone walking amongst the stones. He went back to the bathroom and sat down on the toilet, leaning his head against the wall; the pain was starting to get to him.

You're going into shock, old man, he thought. *There's no one in the graveyard. Hang tight and keep your head straight. Help is on the way.*

Silence hung in the air. After a few minutes, Rhonda asked, "You robbed the bank, didn't you?"

Stephen remained silent.

"I heard that you shot some people."

"So what? Somebody tripped an alarm and suddenly the cops were there. We had no choice," he answered.

"We? You mean you didn't do it yourself?"

"No, my pals Jimmy and Tyler came up from—" Stephen stopped his narrative. "Shut up or I'll shoot you."

"Like you shot that young bank teller and those two police officers?"

"What? How do you know that?" he asked.

"Maybe you should confess. I could be your priest," Rhonda answered.

"Screw that," Stephen said, as he wiped his face. He took a couple of deep breaths to steady himself. *We planned this robbery for a week. How could it go wrong?* he thought.

"I can see your injuries are taking their toll," Rhonda said, sliding the door open. "You should see a doctor."

"Shut up!" Stephen yelled. "I've already shot three people today. If you want to be the fourth, just keep talking."

"You're in shock and not thinking properly. Just like when you shot that poor teller. What did she do to deserve that?"

"I panicked, alright. The gun just went off and I—" Stephen paused. "How do you know any of this?"

"I just know. Just like I know your cell phone is about to ring."

Stephen opened his mouth to speak when the strains of "Breaking the Law" by Judas Priest filled the room. He lay the gun on his lap and pulled out his phone from his jacket pocket. Tyler's name filled the screen, and he hit the answer button.

"Tyler. Where the hell are you? I'm at the house by the graveyard. Come get me."

Silence filled the phone. "Tyler?" Stephen said. Silence.

"It's not Tyler, is it?" Rhonda asked.

Stephen stared at the phone. His hand was shaking.

"Tyler's dead. So is Jimmy, and the two police officers you shot," Rhonda continued. "I bet that's the police confirming you're still alive. I also bet you didn't turn off the tracking app on your phone, did you?"

Stephen dropped the phone and walked to the window in the other bedroom. He saw dozens of ghostly figures in the graveyard walking towards the house. He also heard footsteps on the stairs.

"I have you as a hostage," Stephen said, looking out the window, his voice shaking.

"No, you don't," Rhonda said, as she passed through the tub and walked into the bedroom. As she walked, the house behind her dissolved into a burned-out husk.

"You picked the wrong town to rob. Otherville has a way of balancing out the scales of justice."

Stephen turned to see several ghostly figures enter the burned-out room. They were led by the young teller he'd shot earlier. She wore a blank expression, and, on her shirt, she wore a nametag.

"Tammy Walker," he read the name. Something clicked in his mind as he turned to Rhonda. "Walker. She's…"

"My daughter," Rhonda finished his sentence. Her face grew an enormous smile as her body went completely black. "I died in this house last year. Fire," she paused, as she looked around the room and sighed. 'I've been trying to sell the place ever since."

Stephen's face went slack as Tammy walked up to him.

"You know Tammy, the staging isn't working. We may have to try something else. No one is biting," Rhonda said.

In his mind, he was trying to grasp what was happening in front of him.

They're not real. She's not here. As Tammy leaned in, Stephen's last act in life was to notice Tammy's bright pink lipstick.

As Tammy kissed him on the mouth. Stephen's eyes went wide, and he felt his soul leave his body. His mind screamed in agony.

*

Two hours later, the coroner's staff were carrying Stephen's body out of the house. RCMP Sergeant Lawson watched the men. He stared at the burned-out house, and at the realtor's sign out front, hanging by one hinge. It squeaked in the wind.

"Well?" Lawson asked the coroner, a tall man named Orson as he walked out of the house.

"I would say he died of shock from his injuries," he paused before continuing. "Funny, he was wearing the same colour of lipstick that the young Walker lady used to wear all the time. Neon pink or something like that."

Lawson nodded as Orson got into his van and drove away. He turned to the graveyard and spotted Rhonda Walker walking amongst the headstones. She turned and gave him a knowing look before vanishing into the mist.

A Bad Night at the Inn

Merritton, Ontario, 1880

When Constable Barrett entered the Inn, he smelled death. The mid-afternoon sun came through the windows and illuminated the large room of mostly empty tables. Unlit lanterns hung on the wall, and half-burned candles sat in the middles of the tables.

Barrett, a tall but stout man, walked to the bar and rapped his knuckles on a wooden post. After a few moments, a small, skinny man with grey hair and wire-rimmed glasses entered the room through a door off the bar. He addressed the constable with a smile.

"Good day, Constable, what can I get you?"

"Ale."

The skinny man nodded and filled a tall glass from a barrel underneath the bar. He handed the glass to Barrett, who immediately brought it to his lips. The skinny man watched as the constable soaked his large moustache while he drank the beer. When he was finished, Barrett placed the glass down on the bar and wiped his mouth with his sleeve.

"Thank you," he said, as he passed the skinny man a coin. "Now, are you the innkeeper?"

"Yes," the skinny man answered. "My name is Robert Jacobs. I own this inn, along with my daughter, Penelope."

Barrett nodded. "Your inn is a little distance outside of town. You can't get many visitors."

"We have regulars who come in nightly, as well as visitors who would rather not bring attention to themselves," Jacobs answered.

"Criminals?" Barrett asked, as he motioned for another beer.

"No, maybe just a little bit unusual," Jacobs said, pouring another beer and handing it to Barrett. The constable drank half the beer and placed the glass down on the bar.

"I understand that there was an incident here the other night," Barrett said.

"We have disturbances from time to time. It *is* a drinking establishment," Jacobs said.

Barrett glanced around the inn. Everything was squared away and nothing appeared out of the ordinary. He was about to turn back to his glass of ale when something caught his eye. A large shadow under one of the tables that didn't move with the sun. He walked over and glanced underneath. It was the remnants of a large stain. The colour was red. Barrett stood up and said to Jacobs, "Quite the stain. Are you killing cows in here?"

Jacobs laughed. "No, Constable. That stain is quite old. In fact, I can't remember the incident."

"Dangerous place, your inn," Barrett said, as he strode back to the bar and finished his ale. As he wiped his mouth Barrett added, "By the way, I and my fellow constables have been made aware of a missing person. A Jonathon Cabot. Apparently, a big man. Came off one of the boats as it went through the Welland Canal. He got off at the lock near here and was last heard saying something about getting a decent drink before heading to Toronto. Any ideas?"

Jacobs shook his head.

"Nothing. He didn't stay here, even if he did come in. We've been busy, and I can't keep track of everyone."

Barrett nodded and headed for the door. Before he exited, Barrett turned and spoke. "Busy, eh? From what I understand from the locals, it's been quiet up this way. I suppose though that this Cabot fella could have had a drink elsewhere?"

"Suppose so," Jacobs answered, as he watched the constable leave his inn.

Behind him, the door opened, and his daughter walked in. Penelope was a stark contrast to her father. Tall and fit, with long dark hair and blue eyes, she stood next Jacobs. "Does he suspect anything?"

"He's a constable; he suspects everything. Just keep an eye on our guest."

Penelope grabbed a mug and filled it with ale. As she poured, Jacobs noticed two small bite marks on his daughter's neck. As she left, Jacobs looked at the bloodstain under the table and shuddered.

*

Two nights later, a carriage pulled up in front of the inn. The owner, a tall man with a cape and top hat, stepped out of the carriage and threw five coins at his driver.

"Go into the town and find four stout men with shovels. I have a feeling we may have to bury some of our troubles."

The driver tipped his hat and engaged the horses. The carriage owner walked up to the inn and noticed the sign.

"The Moose and Owl."

He opened the door and stepped inside.

A roaring fire lit the room along with several lamps hanging on hooks. A haze of smoke blurred the faces of the occupants. The carriage owner walked around the full tables towards the bar. Jacobs noticed the man.

"Good evening, Sir. What can I trouble you for?"

"Beer."

As Jacobs poured the beer, the carriage owner looked around the room. Most of the men were playing cards or telling exaggerated stories. There was only one woman in the room, and she was in the back, talking to a tall man dressed in a white shirt and black pants. When the beer was poured, the carriage owner addressed Jacobs.

"Busy night."

"Tonight, yes. Usually, it's only a couple of men from the town, however, there are a few boats this evening at the Port. These men came from the east coast to find work along the canal. I think some of the interviews are being conducted in here."

"I see. Thanks for the beer," he said, dropping a coin on the bar and bringing the glass to his lips. "My name is

Richards, Calvin Richards. My job is to investigate unusual occurrences."

Jacobs nodded and poured another beer. The young lady at the back walked up, grabbed the beer, and brought it to another table.

"It seems your Constable Barrett had gotten some information about a missing person, and it also seems his recent disappearance is shrouded in mystery."

"I don't know much, except he may have been here and left."

Richards stroked his full beard. His piercing green eyes shot through Jacobs, who shrank a little. Richards moved to pick up his beer but instead, lashed out and grabbed Jacobs. He pulled the bartender towards him and whispered in his ear.

"I know about the blood stain under the table. Barrett told me. I also know about that stranger in the back who's been flirting with your daughter. Well, that stranger has a knack of finding trouble, and I'm the one who must deal with it."

Jacobs struggled against the bar as Richards' voice became more sinister.

"Now, Cabot died in here the other night, didn't he?"

Jacobs looked away.

"Tell me, or so help me, it will be on your daughter's head."

Jacobs hesitated, then slowly nodded his head. Richards smiled.

"Where is the body?"

"Buried over the hill. We took his money, but buried him with all his documents."

"How did he die?"

"The stranger was protecting my daughter from him."

"Thank you. That was easy," Richards said, as he finished his beer. He asked for two more beers, paid the bill and took both beers with him to the back of the room. The stranger looked up at Richards, who placed both beers on the table and had a seat.

"Mr. O'Dell, it's nice to see you. It's been a while."

O'Dell grabbed the beer and took a drink. Richards pressed on. "It seems death follows you around. This inn is no exception."

O'Dell kept quiet. Richards smiled.

"Did you really think catching a boat to a bigger country than Ireland would hide you from me? It was still easy to find you. I just followed the trail of bodies."

"I didn't kill anyone," O'Dell said.

"Ah, but Death follows you around, doesn't he? He's like an old friend, a travelling companion, an old mate. So, tell me, how did this Cabot bastard die?"

O'Dell said nothing, but drank more of his beer. Richards sat back in his chair and studied the man. His long brown hair, which matched his eyes, hung to his shoulders. He was fit, and no doubt could have any woman he wanted. Richards took a drink and pressed further.

"The bartender says Cabot died because he was threatening the daughter. She *is* quite pretty. I noticed her when she came to the bar. She also had two bite marks on her neck. Reminded me of that sweet lass in Dubin. Siobhan, that was her name."

O'Dell's face saddened for a moment.

"She had bite marks on her neck. The local police suggested it was a sex thing. Crime of passion, O'Dell?" Richards leaned in. "Did she enjoy it?"

O'Dell sat still and didn't answer. Richards took another drink. The laughter from the other tables engulfed the room for a minute, and O'Dell wished he was a part of it. He hung his head, closed his eyes, and let out a long breath.

"Siobhan was a vampire."

Richards paused in his drinking.

"Vampires like to be bitten on the neck during sex. It excites them. They sometimes like the feeling of being the victim."

"Before they feed?" Richards asked.

"No, Vampires don't feed every day. They can go weeks without feeding. Cabot was just in the wrong place. He grabbed young Penelope and…it happened."

Richards pulled a pistol from beneath his cape and pointed it O'Dell.

"Let's say for the moment that I believe you. Who killed Siobhan?"

"A man named Hugo," O'Dell answered.

Richards laughed. He stood up and pointed the pistol at O'Dell's chest.

"O'Dell, you are a liar and killer." He pulled back the hammer. "Prepare to meet your friend, Death."

As he pulled the trigger, Richards felt a shock of pain in his neck. He dropped his pistol, but O'Dell was out of his seat and caught it before it hit the floor. As he struggled, Richards caught his reflection in the side window. Penelope was devouring his neck. He felt his legs give out from under him. Soon he was on the floor, feeling his life's energy leaving his body.

Penelope stood and stared at the other patrons who were watching the scene. Her mouth and her white dress were stained with blood. Some of the patrons were rising, ready to intervene. Penelope shook out her hair, and her eyes turned red. The patrons stood silently.

"Gentlemen," she said, "it seems that our bartender is offering everyone a free drink. Help yourselves to the bar."

The crowd stood still for a moment, before cheering and heading to the bar, where Jacobs was already pouring. O'Dell dragged Richards' body outside, while Penelope started to clean up. Outside, O'Dell encountered the carriage driver and four men with shovels. The driver leapt from the carriage at the sight of his boss.

"My good Lord, what has happened to him?"

Before O'Dell could answer, one of the men hit the driver over the head with his shovel. The driver hit the ground, his frozen face full of confusion. One of the other men walked forward, touched the driver's neck, and nodded to the others. Before O'Dell could speak, a third man said, "We always keep our secrets away from the village."

"Don't worry," the fourth man said, as he grabbed the driver by the ankles. "No one will find them or the carriage."

"The horses?" O'Dell asked.

"Plenty of farms around here who could use a couple of good horses, and these are in wonderful shape," the first man answered

"Others will come," O'Dell said. "What will happen then?"

The four men shrugged and carried on with disposing the bodies. A few minutes later, the carriage pulled away with a new driver. O'Dell watched them leave, and soon the night became silent. He breathed in the cool air and collected himself. When he was ready, O'Dell returned to the inn just as Penelope had finished cleaning up.

She smiled at him as she returned to her duties. O'Dell took a seat, and watched the patrons, who carried on as if nothing had happened. Hours later, when he was sharing his bed with Penelope, he wondered out loud about other visitors.

"They will come. Richards was well-known to the hunters."

"If they come, they come," was her response. "Just accept it and enjoy what moments you have free from Death."

O'Dell nodded and allowed Penelope her desires.
Happiness was a stranger to him, he thought, but in this place,
he could make it his friend.

The Lock

Daniel Chamberlain cursed his boss, the weather, and the time as he stepped out of his car. He popped the trunk and retrieved his diving gear. As he made his way towards the side gate at the edge of the lock, his boss, Sandra Olsen gave him a half-hearted smile.

"Sorry to drag you out at this hour, Daniel, but we have an emergency."

"Yes, it seems all the emergencies happen at two in the morning," Daniel said, as he started to pull on his diving gear. "This had better be some kind of major emergency."

"It is," Sandra said. "Daniel, let me introduce you to Mr. Fox."

Daniel turned and noticed the man for the first time. He was tall, dressed in all black, with a long black coat. His hair was long and bordered his long black beard. He was the opposite of Sandra, who even at two in the morning, looked like she had done her hair and picked out her best outfit.

Daniel took Fox's hand and shook it. It felt strange. Fox nodded and spoke in a low voice. "I understand your frustration, Daniel, but my ship is just cycling out of Lock 4 and will be here shortly. We need to make sure that the Lock 3 is clear and free."

"Sorry for asking, but what kind of special needs does your ship have that necessitate me diving into the canal?"

"Sorry, I cannot say. Just be assured that it does have special needs."

Daniel regarded Mr. Fox with a questionable look. Fox turned to Sandra.

"I must return to my ship. I will meet it at the bridge."

Before Sandra could acknowledge the man, Mr. Fox was already through the side gate and heading up the canal pathway. As Daniel struggled into his wet suit, a memory nagged at him. Something his great Uncle Peter had mentioned to him. Something to do with an incident on a train heading through Quebec. He shook the partial memory away and finished getting dressed.

When he stepped to the edge of the gates, Daniel noticed a couple of people on the viewing platform that connected the St. Catharines Museum and the Welland Canal Centre. Daniel recognized them as ship spotters. Fox's ship must be one of those rare vessels that would get ship-obsessed photographers out of bed at this ungodly hour.

Daniel sat down at the edge of the canal and put on his flippers. Sandra helped him with his SCUBA tank, and he put on his mask with headlamp. Before he slid into the water, she added, "Just a quick look, Daniel. Make sure all is good, and come straight up again."

Daniel nodded, and heard the siren for the Glendale bridge. He turned and saw the lift bridge starting to rise, with Fox's ship coming up to it. He put the respirator in his mouth and slid into water.

The weighted belt slowly brought Daniel down into the murky water. He was next to the open fifty-foot gates at the south end of the lock. Daniel marvelled at the engineering. As he glanced around, he also thought about the funny way the Welland Canal cut across the Niagara Escarpment. When ships went up the Canal, you were heading south; going down meant north.

As he touched down on the rocky bottom, Daniel turned on his headlamp. He quickly glanced at the gates and saw nothing that would inhibit the ship from coming through. He jumped up and swam towards the lock. Though lit from the top, the last thirty or so feet of the lock were black and foreboding.

As he swam towards it, Daniel heard a low growl. He shook his head. He dismissed the sound and kept going. As he passed through the gates, a second growl came out of the darkness, and Daniel pulled up. He glanced around at the cracked concrete, searching for a possible source for the sound. He saw nothing. He also thought about getting out, as Fox's ship would be getting close.

As he swam towards the west side of the lock, Daniel heard the growl again. Glancing down, his heart nearly leapt out of his chest as he saw two large glowing eyes stare up at him.

Christ Jesus! his mind screamed as he leaned back and kicked his feet frantically. As he made his way back through the gates, a large head emerged from the darkness. It was snake-like, and attached to a large Komodo dragon-shaped body. A large right appendage with a giant claw grabbed the edge of the lock.

As he swam, Daniel glanced up and, to his horror, Fox's ship appeared out of the gloom. He turned back to see the creature had both claws on the edge and was staring at him, a grim smile on its face as a forked tongue slithered out of its mouth.

Turning back to the ship, Daniel noticed the bulbous bow cracking open.

"What the hell?" he thought, as the crack in the bow widened. He heard the creature growl again, which spurred him into action. He swam to the canal wall. The ship was just coming off the side of the canal as it lined up to enter the lock. Daniel realized the remaining space along the side was too small for him.

"Shit!" Daniel glanced up and saw the ship's anchor. He shot upwards as fast as could kick. As he reached out to the giant hook, he heard the roar of the creature. He kicked up once more and grabbed the anchor, throwing his arms and legs around the hook as the creature lunged towards him. He closed his eyes in terror, awaiting his fate.

Nothing happened. He opened his eyes to see the creature's tail disappear into a hatch in the bow of the ship, which closed as the ship entered the lock. Daniel held on to the anchor as ship passed through the gates with about a foot-and-a-half gap. His tank scraped along the concrete wall.

Daniel held his breath as he glanced up and saw the lights of the platform, trying to calculate where he was in the lock. He was about halfway through when he felt the ship slow down. He glanced forward and saw the ship arrestor cable in front of him. As the ship slowed, Daniel pushed off the anchor and kicked hard towards the cable.

He could feel the boat behind him as he stretched out and grabbed the steel coating. He quickly pulled his head out of the water.

"Daniel!" he heard Sandra yelling, as he turned to see his boss running down the edge of the lock. He pulled himself along the cable to the edge. Sandra helped him out as he heard the alarms for the south gate. He climbed out of the water in time to see the gates close.

"What the hell happened down there?" she asked.

Coughing and sputtering, Daniel ripped off his respirator, caught his breath and replied, "Why don't you ask your buddy, Fox? He used me as bait, and I nearly got eaten!"

"Eaten? What do you mean eaten?"

"There was a bloody huge monster down there. Didn't you see the front of the ship open?"

Sandra stood there, dumbfounded. Daniel grabbed his gear and started to walk back towards the gate. As he passed by the ship, he spotted Fox standing on the port side. He tipped his hat to Daniel.

"You bastard!" Daniel yelled. "You knew that thing was down there, and you let me go down anyway."

Fox stood silent for a moment. He nodded and replied, "Yes, but you were in no danger. Once it reared its head, we had a beacon for it to follow. We just needed it to come up."

"Didn't help that I was nearly crushed by your ship."

"We were aware of your situation. As I said, you were never in danger."

Daniel scoffed, and yelled more obscenities at Fox. As he turned to walk away, Daniel heard Fox yell to him, "I knew your great-uncle. Sgt Chamberlain was a good man who also helped me out of a couple of situations."

Daniel turned back to Fox, who nodded again and walked down a set of steps into the cargo hold. Daniel waited for the ship to cycle through the lock, and was glad to see the back end of it sail through the north gates. As he walked to his car, Sandra caught up to him.

"Daniel, I'm sorry if this was upsetting for you, but come on—there wasn't a monster down there. It was probably a trick of the light."

"That was no trick of the light. You can't convince me otherwise. Now, I'm going home and having a large drink, seeing how I was nearly killed."

Daniel placed the last of his gear in the trunk. He shook his head at Sandra, got into his car, and drove away. Later, after he got home, Daniel pulled out an old photo album of his great-uncle, Sgt Chamberlain. Inside was a picture of him and his squad before they boarded the train to Halifax.

Daniel remembered him telling a story about some creature on a train, and a strange encounter in France. Daniel also remembered him mentioning a Mr. Fox. He shook his head and grabbed a beer. It would be several beers before the horrors of the night were pushed away.

*

Sandra watched Daniel go. As she walked back to her own car, her phone rang. She answered and recognized the voice.

"It's OK. No one is going to believe him anyway. I know him, he'll be on a bender for a couple of days. It's why his wife left him, being drunk a lot of the time. I'll visit him later in the week and convince him it didn't happen. Nothing to worry about, Mr. Fox."

Satisfied, Fox hung up, and Sandra got into her car. Driving home, Sandra thought it might have been easier if Daniel was crushed by the ship. The witnesses on the platform would say it was an accident. She glanced in her rearview mirror. There were similarities between Daniel's wife and herself. That could work—Daniel was a good-looking man.

"The things we do for these unnatural travelers," Sandra said as she drove home.

The Fisherman

Whale's Cove, Newfoundland, 1999

The children danced and played in the living room to the sounds of fiddles and accordions coming from the record player. Laughter and voices from the parents echoed off the walls in the kitchen. The pot of fish and brews, along with the salt beef, filled the air with salivating smells, tantalizing the tastebuds of the guests. Everywhere in the house, happiness dominated.

In the back corner of the living room, oblivious to the laughter and smells, an old man sat in his rocking chair. Dressed in a worn flannel checkerboard shirt, grey slacks and wool socks, the man with salt and pepper hair and harsh blue eyes watched his small TV as it showcased the latest out-of-shape men wrestling for a chance at a fictional world title. At ninety-three years old, Mason O'Leary couldn't walk very well or hold his own fork and knife. Arthritis had crippled the former fisherman and reduced him to shell of his former self.

Instead of regaling the youngsters who danced to jigs and reels with tales of his exploits on the water, Mason sought refuge in wrestling and his 'stories', soap operas from the States. As his family celebrated the birth of Mason's fourth great-grandson, the old man felt isolated and forgotten in his world of fictional heroes.

The chest pain started as the wrestling heel pinned the babyface and won the World title. Mason grunted at the TV in rage. Soon the pain in his chest took his breath away and he started drooling. He convulsed his chair and started to slide down. It was only when he hit the floor did one of the dancing children notice Mason and run to the kitchen.

"Poppy fell out of his chair!" the young girl of 7 told the room filled with adults. John O'Leary, Mason's son, put down his beer and ran to the living room. As he knelt next to Mason, John asked, "Pop, what's the matter?"

"Chest!" was all that Mason could get out.

When John mentioned taking Mason to the hospital, Mason protested. He didn't trust doctors. After much commotion, John and three of his brothers carried Mason up to bed. John helped Mason take his heart medication and covered him up. Mason thanked his son, and assured him that he would be alright. John left his father and returned to the celebration.

Hours later, when the celebration died off and family members left for their own homes. Mason's only daughter Mary, the youngest of his children, checked on him before heading to bed herself. Mason looked up at her beautiful face, bordered by long brown hair which had a tinge of grey, and smiled.

"I only wish that Brian was here," he said to her.

Mary looked down at her father. She pulled her black shawl over her shoulders and hitched up her skirt to sit on the bed.

"Oh Pop, Uncle Brian passed away four years ago."

Mason went silent. He gazed up at the ceiling as Mary took his hand and caressed it. After a while, she got up and kissed Mason on the cheek. "Sleep well. Tomorrow I'll get that syrup you like from the market."

Mary got up, straightened her pleated skirt, and walked out of the room. Mason lay on his bed staring at the ceiling. As he lay there, the events of over sixty years ago entered his mind. He was instantly taken back.

Whale's Cove, 1936

The light of the full moon shone into the bedroom as Mason opened his eyes. The hands on the wall clock showed 3:30. He rolled over and looked at his wife Grace, heavy with child, sleeping soundly. He gave her a light peck on the cheek before getting out of bed. Mason pulled on his long johns, wool socks and shirt, followed by his grey pants and red flannel overshirt. He silently went downstairs to the kitchen and donned his rubber boots and oil skins.

From the icebox, Mason took two sandwiches wrapped in cloth, and put them into his lunch bag. He ate a small breakfast of toast and tea and, after clearing the dishes, walked out the front door towards the docks.

The full moon shone down on the little town, illuminating the greens, browns, and yellows of the houses. Mason gazed at the stars and smiled. This was the best time of day. Other fishermen in the town wouldn't be up for another hour, and Mason like the peace and quiet.

Mason walked past the old bell that was used for signalling emergencies, and down to the dock. He climbed into his boat, untying it from the dock, and rowed out to his nets.

Mason's area was about a mile out. With the calm seas, he would make good time. Mason pulled against the slight waves, and within an hour, spotted his buoy.

Hooking up to his marker, Mason started the job of pulling in his nets. Slowly but surely, the cod filled his boat like gold from the ocean. As he hauled the fish in, Mason thought about a new winter's coat for Grace that she could order from the Sears magazine. The baby's needs were looked after, thanks to his brother Robert, who had made a wooden crib in his workshop, and to Grace's sisters for making the baby clothes. Mason felt content and happy.

As he pulled in his net, Mason felt something catch. Reaching over the gunnels, Mason gripped the net and touched a hand. He reeled back from the shock. A couple of moments later, Mason looked tentatively over the side.

The hand belonged to a man, but it was different. The hand was grey with six fingers. Slowly maneuvering the net, Mason heaved the man into the boat. He had a bald head, with big eyes and a small mouth, and slits for a nose. He was grey all over, with a small covering over his private area.

It was like no other man Mason had ever encountered. The sight reminded him of a story Bill Strong had told the other day about a bright light shooting across the sky three nights ago, just over Whale's Cove. Being a drunk, no one believed him. As Mason looked down at the man lying amongst his cod, he saw some credence in Bill's story. The man's chest rose slightly and regularly. Satisfied that the man would live, Mason finished bringing in his catch and baiting the net. Once his work was done, Mason released his net and turned his boat towards the shore.

As he rowed for shore, Mason waved to his neighbours as they made their way to their own nets. The sun was just under the horizon when he reached the dock. After securing his boat, Mason grabbed a blanket from under his bag and covered up the man. Looking around and thinking it was safe, Mason pulled the man from his boat and carried him home.

Grace was in the kitchen in her nightgown preparing breakfast when Mason opened the door, carried the man in and sat him in a kitchen chair. It took Mason a couple of minutes to explain what happened. Grace knelt next to the man and took his hand. Closing her eyes, she was able to feel the strength of their guest.

Grace, born on the west coast of the island, had been, as her mother would describe it, 'blessed with *it*'. A sort of sixth sense about the world. She could tell when someone close had died, could communicate with the recently deceased in a limited way, and always knew when trouble was brewing. Now she felt the man, and knew he would be alright. Mason trusted that Grace would be safe with the stranger, and left to finish with the fish.

Two hours later, with a day's wage in his pocket, Mason returned home to a weird sight. Sitting at his kitchen table were Grace and the man. He was sipping tea and had a slight smile on his face. Grace was laughing when she spotted Mason.

"He doesn't talk like us. It's through your head that he speaks."

Mason nodded and looked at the man, who stared back at him. Suddenly, Mason heard words in his head.

Thank you. I believe you saved me.

Mason nodded and turned to Grace who was smiling, then took off his boots and oilskins. He grabbed a cup from the cupboard, poured himself some tea, and joined them.

Over the next few days, the grey man rested in the small spare room at the back and ate only morsels. When Mason inquired, Grace informed him that their guest ate sparingly, but on a regular basis.

"In fact, I think I'm overfeeding him."

Two mornings later, when Mason came downstairs, he saw the grey man standing in the kitchen waiting for him.

I wanted to thank you by coming out and helping you with your work.

Mason nodded and smiled. He went into the back closet and retrieved his old oilskins and boots. Ten minutes later, the grey man was suited up and walking with Mason down the road.

"By the way, you've been with us a couple of days and we don't know your name. If you don't mind telling me."

The grey man thought for a minute before answering in Mason's mind.

I really don't know if I have a name. Never had the need for one. I heard Grace mention a Brian when she was talking to someone at the door. She called him 'Our Brian'.

"Oh yes, Brian Smith. That's her brother who lives in Corner Brook. He works at the mill."

Could you call me Brian since it would remind Grace of her brother?

Mason smiled, and said as they approached the docks, "Brian it is."

An hour later, he and Brian were pulling in nets, dumping the fish, and rebaiting. Brian needed very little instruction, and the work was done quickly. They even had time to jig for some fish. Mason could hear Brian's laughter in his head.

Fishing is fun. Have you always fished? Brian asked.

"It's the only thing I know how to do. It's in our blood, and if you ask me, it's the best job in the world. Especially after a good morning, it's great to head home and join Grace at the table," Mason answered. "I think I will fish to the moment I die."

The morning sun was creeping up from the horizon as the two friends made for the shore. They were halfway in when Mason asked, "Brian, I didn't want to mention this before but, where is your home?"

Brian looked to the sky and pointed. A sadness came to his eyes. *A long way, and more than a day's journey.*

Mason looked to the sky as well, and felt his sadness. He himself had joined the Royal Newfoundland Regiment when he turned fifteen towards the end of the war. He made it to England but never saw battle. He was remembering how homesick he was when Brian, reading his mind, spoke to him.

You're lucky you came home. I take it some didn't.

Mason nodded. Wiping away the tears, he said, "I lost two brothers and a cousin in the war. The war was so far away and yet it touched so many of us."

Brian went silent as they continued towards the shore. Mason was grateful to Brian for allowing him a few minutes of grief. Brian felt the heaviness of it.

As they approached the docks, many of the other fishermen were bringing up their catch to be weighed and sold. The fish merchant looked happy at the haul. Mason turned to Brian and said quietly, "Now look Brian, people around here may be a little taken aback by your appearance. They don't know you like Grace and I do. So, do as I say, keep your head down and, if possible, keep your hands in your pockets."

Brian agreed and understood. They pulled up to the fish merchant and unloaded. The merchant, James Pretty, a tall and well-dressed man, checked his paperwork while the men worked. When the haul was weighed, James Pretty glanced at the reading, did the accounting and paid Mason. He didn't even look at Brian.

Mason and Brian went back to the boat and cast off. Soon they were in Mason's berth and tying up. Mason nodded to Brian.

"Good job, me ducky."

Brian smiled. They finished up their work and headed back to the house. They were about halfway home when they heard a commotion. A fire had broken out on one of the fish stages.

"Come on!" Mason yelled to Brian. "If that spreads, all the wharves will go up in flames."

The two friends ran to the shoreline where a few men where already filling buckets of water. They quickly joined in and were soon trudging heavy buckets up the fishing stage. Soon the whole town was out watching the mayhem; women in shawls and children were running out with their rubber boots half on.

An hour later, the men of Whale's Cove finished putting the fire out. The stage was a blackened shell of its former self. Peter Finlay looked at his stage and sighed. He turned to the crowd and spoke:

"Thank you. Thanks to all of you, my buddies. I don't know what I would have done without you."

"We'll rebuild her," Seamus O'Donnell, another fisherman said, patting Peter on the back. "At least no one got hurt."

Peter was about to say something to Seamus when he paused and stared at the crowd. Everyone turned to see what he was staring at. It was Brian. During the commotion, Brian's hat had fallen off. Some of the women put their hands to their mouths. Some of the small children screamed and ran home. Some of the older boys picked up rocks and started to throw them at Brian.

"What in the name of Jesus is *that?*" Peter yelled. The crowd turned ugly and started to shout at Brian.

Mason stepped in front of his friend and protected him from the rocks. As the rocks hit him, Brian said to Mason, *I'm sorry. I didn't mean to lose my hat.*

"You've got nothing to be sorry for, my friend. Nothing at all."

As the rocks and insults flew towards the two men, the emergency bell sounded. Everyone turned to see Grace, wearing only her housecoat and slippers, beating on the bell with a hammer.

When the crowd went quiet, she roared, "If my mother were alive today, she'd be shocked at the lot of you! Peter Finlay! That man helped save your stage and *this* is how you repay him? If *your* mother was here, she would be ashamed of you and give you a right smack across the back of the head. As for the rest of you, where are your hearts? Father Johnson at the church says we need to love all God's creatures."

The crowd went silent. Mason stepped forward.

"I found Brian out in the water, nearly dead. I brought him ashore, and Grace nursed him back to health. This morning, he helped with the fishing, and just now, he helped with the fire. He's a good soul. You can trust him."

"But he looks so different," an older boy said.

"So? There are all sorts of different people in the world," Mason replied. But before he continued, a shout was heard from the burned stage.

"Help! It's Joe Stevens. He's not breathing!" a young man dressed in oilskins yelled out.

Several men, along with Mason and Brian, ran to the stage. Joe was only slightly burned but not breathing. His face was turning blue.

"He was out cod fishing with me this morning," Peter said. "Joe, can you hear me?"

Suddenly, a voice came to the men in their heads.

Please, step away. I can help him.

The men backed away as Brian stepped forward. He knelt next to Joe and put his six-fingered hand on Joe's chest. A small grey glow emerged from his hand, and suddenly Joe started to cough. He slowly opened his eyes. The townsfolk stared in awe at Brian as Joe was helped up.

Peter stepped forward and spoke. "Thank you, Brian. Thank you. I'm sorry. Truly sorry." Tears sprang from his eyes as he spoke. The crowd stepped forward, and someone started to clap. Soon, the whole town was cheering. Brian stared past the crowd and gazed upon Mason and Grace, who were smiling.

*

It was in the middle of the night a month later when a bright light shone upon Whale's Cove. The townsfolk gathered to see the sight.

Brian touched Grace's forehead and spoke. *Thank you again. You will have five beautiful children and a full life.*

Grace hugged him and wished him luck. Brian turned back to Mason and said quietly, *Thank you for saving my life. You are a good friend, and I will see you again.*

With that, Brian rose into the air towards the light. When he disappeared, the light vanished, and the memory of Brian was erased from the townsfolk's memories—all except for Mason and Grace.

*

Mason was awakened by a strange sound in his head.

How are you my old friend?"

Mason opened his eyes. Standing in front of him was Brian. He sat down on Mason's bed and touched his hands.

"My end is almost here, old buddy," Mason said.

I know, but I am here for a different reason.

Brian touched Mason's head, and suddenly, the two of them were in Mason's boat, the full moon in the sky. "We have until sunrise," Brian said.

Mason looked at his hands and saw that the arthritis was gone. He smiled at Brian and together they hauled in the net. Mason laughed as they worked. "Do you think we have time for some jigging?" Mason asked.

Brian smiled, which told Mason that they did.

Working Them Angels

"Come now, Mr. Carter, tell us how it's done, and this nonsense will be all over."

Stephen Carter opened his good eye and looked at the speaker. He wore a dark suit with a matching fedora. His goatee had grey patches while the rest of his hair was pure black. He was sitting beside a small table, drinking tea.

Stephen, however, was the opposite. He was half-naked and hanging by his wrists, his toes just touching the floor. He was covered in sweat and blood. One eye was swollen shut, and his nose and lips were crimson. Every inch of his body ached.

"I don't know how to do it. Like I said before, I don't even know what you're talking about."

With a nod from the speaker, a fist came out of nowhere and smashed into his ribs. Stephen felt something crack. He moaned and closed the other eye. The impact of the punch caused him to swing from his wrists.

Sighing, the speaker took a sip of tea and studied Carter. He nodded to the owner of the fist, a tall muscular man, who grabbed Stephen and arrested his swinging. The speaker stood up and walked over to his prisoner. Stephen could smell his breath before he spoke.

"Let me ask you a question. Do you know what's at stake?"

Stephen shook his head.

"The battle for this way of life. A war is coming, and to fight that war, you need soldiers. Now, the interested parties I represent have plenty of soldiers—well, more fighters than soldiers. However, to win a war, you *also* need intelligence on how the other side works."

The speaker paused, waiting for Stephen to interject. When he didn't, the speaker carried on.

"Now, the intelligence we need relates to controlling the soldiers from the other side. You have that ability, and it's been witnessed."

Stephen lifted his head at that statement. "Witnessed?"

"The fatal accident you and your wife somehow survived. It was caught on a cell phone camera. A white phantom pushing your car out of the way and into a light pole. The car was written off, but you both survived."

Stephen remembered the accident. Some idiots had run a red light and were about to broadside his car on the passenger side. At the last second, Stephen's car swerved and avoided the accident. He and his wife, Tanya, were shaken up but alive.

"There was also the incident of the earthquake in Japan. When it struck, you and your wife were on the balcony of your hotel. When it cracked, your wife fell, and you reached out and grabbed her hand. You struggled to hang on. Just as your grip slipped, your wife was miraculously pushed up onto the balcony."

Stephen closed his eye. He remembered the fear on Tanya's face as she started to slip from his fingers. He couldn't believe what happened. One second, she was falling; the next she was lying next to him, crying. He held her tight as the quake petered out.

"Bloody cell phones are everywhere. This phone caught a white phantom swooping in at the last second and saving your wife. That's two incidents, Stephen."

Stephen lifted his head again. The speaker wore a concerned smile.

"Stephen, time is running out. Please, end your suffering and tell us what we need to know. I don't want to drag this out any longer."

Stephen wore a look of desperation. He shook his head and spoke. "I don't know what you want. This is the first I've ever heard of these phantoms. I can't explain it."

The speaker turned to his accomplice and nodded towards a door at the end of the room. The big man walked over and knocked three times. The door opened, and a small, but no less fit man stood there in the doorway. Stephen could hear them talking but couldn't make out what they were saying.

After a minute, the big man returned with two others behind him, carrying an unconscious figure secured to a chair. Stephen gasped as the men put the chair down in front of him. It was Tanya. As he stared at his wife, Stephen remembered what had happened.

It was their anniversary. He was looking dapper in his best blue suit, waiting for her in front of the restaurant. At the appointed time, a taxi pulled up next to him. He strode over, paid the driver, and opened the back door. Tanya stepped out of a dream. She was dressed in the finest red pantsuit, with matching long black boots, a wool coat with fur collar, and a designer hat.

Stephen was gobsmacked, and Tanya smiled at his reaction. It was exactly what she wanted. He stepped forward and kissed her cheek. As he turned to lead her to the restaurant, Stephen heard Tanya gasp. He spun around to see a stranger holding a cloth over Tanya's mouth, while a black van pulled up beside them. Stephen ran towards the assailant only to be tasered from behind.

Stephen was immersed in pain. He fell to the ground convulsing. Before he passed out, he saw the men load Tanya into the van. Now, she was tied to the chair in front of him. Tape was across her mouth. Her hat was gone, and her dark hair was dishevelled.

"Stephen, I'm sorry it's come to this but, since you won't tell us how it works, maybe using our gentle techniques on your wife will make you a little more forthcoming."

"Please, we don't know anything about these phantoms," Stephen blurted out.

The speaker shook his head. "You know, Stephen, I really hoped that it wouldn't come to this. Your wife is quite striking. I would hate to disfigure her because of your stubbornness."

"I don't know anything!" Stephen shouted.

The speaker looked sympathetic as he pulled out a cell phone and dialed a number.

"Yes, I need you," the speaker said into the phone. He hung up and sat down. The waiting was tortuous to Stephen. He was glad Tanya was still unconscious. The speaker continued to sip his tea as his henchmen sat in silence.

There was a knock at the door. The big man walked over and answered it. A small bald man with a large moustache walked into the room carrying a briefcase. He nodded to the speaker before opening the briefcase on the small table. Stephen stared in horror.

The briefcase contained knives of all shapes and sizes, as well as various other cutting tools. The blades were shiny and reflected the low light in the room.

"Now, let me introduce you to Mr. Chow. I know, he doesn't look Asian; in truth, he just likes the name."

Mr. Chow turned and bowed. His smile betrayed an enthusiasm for his work.

"Now, seeing as you won't tell us anything, we will see what beautiful Tanya has to say."

Stephen cried out but was silenced by a dirty rag that was shoved into this mouth. Mr. Chow walked over to Tanya and waved some smelling salts under her nose. She woke up with a start and took in her surroundings. She tried to scream through her gag and struggled to get out of the chair.

Mr. Chow walked back to his briefcase as the two henchmen held Tanya down in the chair. Stephen strained against his bindings. The speaker sat in his chair sipping his tea, as Mr. Chow put on a show of pulling out several knives and caressing them in a loving manner. Eventually, the little man pulled out a pair of pruning shears.

Stephen kicked out at Mr. Chow. The little man stepped aside and taunted him with the garden tool. With all his remaining strength, Stephen started to swing himself towards the group. His wrists were screaming. As he swung forward, kicking his legs, he was met by the large man, who punched him once more in the stomach.

The wind disappeared from his lungs. Stephen managed to spit out the cloth in his mouth as he desperately tried to regain his breath back. The large man stopped Stephen's momentum and held him in place. The speaker smiled at Stephen.

"I love your determination, Stephen, but this is going to happen." After a pause, he continued, "Mr. Chow, no more standing on ceremony; get to it."

Mr. Chow nodded and walked behind Tanya's chair where her hands were tied. Stephen saw the fear in her eyes. Mr. Chow grabbed the pinky finger of Tanya's right hand. He placed the blades of the shears at the base of the finger. Tanya screamed through the gag and tried to pull away. The two henchmen held her in place.

The speaker stood up. He walked over to Tanya and pulled the tape off her mouth. Tanya sucked in air as the speaker put his face in front of hers. In a quiet voice he said, "Please, just tell us how this works, and you and Stephen are free to go. No more pain. No more torture. Just walk away and you won't be bothered again. I really don't want to hurt you."

Tanya looked at the speaker with her bright blue eyes. She swallowed, and in a soft and defeated whisper, she said, "I don't know."

The speaker looked at Tanya as tears started to flow down her face. The speaker nodded and glanced at Mr. Chow. Stephen saw the gleam of excitement in Chow's eyes. He turned his attention to Tanya, who was staring at him, and gave her the most loving look he had.

Chow squeezed the handle slightly, so the blades rested against the leather of Tanya's glove. She jumped at the sensation. Stephen saw the evil smile on Chow's face as he leaned close to Tanya's ear.

"I smell your fear, little lady; it excites me," Chow said, licking the back of Tanya's ear. She grunted in disgust. Chow continued, "My mother, you see, once told me that you must find something in life that you're good at and enjoy. Well, I enjoy causing pain and I'm quite good at it." After a slight pause, he said, "So, say goodbye to your little piggy."

Chow clamped a hand over Tanya's mouth. Stephen screamed out and Tanya's eyes went wide. As Chow began to squeeze the handle, a large bang sounded across the room. Everyone paused and looked up. A second bang echoed off the walls. Chow released Tanya and stood looking at the speaker, confused. The speaker nodded to the huge henchman, who walked over to the door.

Stephen twisted himself to gaze at Tanya, who was in a trance. The speaker, Mr. Chow, and the other two henchmen stood facing the door. As the huge henchman reached out for the handle, the door flew off its hinges and smashed into his face.

The huge henchman fell to the ground, dead, as the door landed on him. Everyone stared in horror as a tall and muscular pale man walked into the room. He was naked, except for a covering over his private parts.

The speaker turned back to Tanya, who was still in a trance, and smiled. He turned back to his other henchmen and ordered, "Just don't stand there, shoot him!"

The two smaller henchmen strode towards the tall man, pulling out their handguns. The tall man stood his ground as the two men fired. The bullets disappeared as they struck the tall man in his chest to no effect. The two henchmen looked at each other, then emptied their magazines. In a flash, the tall man was standing in front of them.

They stared up at the tall man, who reached out and grabbed each of them by the neck, lifting the two men off the ground and squeezing. The men's eyes burst out of their heads. The tall man dropped the two bodies and walked towards Mr. Chow.

Chow retreated to his briefcase and pulled out his biggest knife. He ran back and held the knife across Tanya's throat.

"I'll kill her, you angelic bastard!" he yelled, as he drew the knife across her throat. Stephen screamed. Chow stood up and pointed the knife at the tall man, who slowly walked forward. As Chow waved the knife, he noticed there was no blood on it. He turned back to Tanya. Her throat was untouched.

Confused, Mr. Chow looked at his knife. As he turned, Chow was met with a punch to the chest, causing his lungs to implode. The knife clanged against the floor. The tall man bent down and picked it up. As Chow staggered, the tall man slammed the knife into his throat. Chow's eyes rolled into his head and he fell to the ground.

The speaker was standing behind his table, sipping his tea. He put the cup down and cracked his neck. To the tall pale man, he said, "Enough seraphim. You know who I am, and unless you want to start something bigger than the both of us, leave now."

The tall man paused and glared at the speaker. After a moment, he walked over to Stephen. He grabbed the bound man by the waist with both hands and pulled straight down. Stephen screamed as his wrists slid out of the restraints, broken. He hit the floor with a thud.

The tall man turned back to the speaker and snapped his fingers. The ropes binding Tanya to the chair fell away. She jumped up and ran to Stephen, kneeling next to him and cradling his head.

The speaker smiled at the couple. He tipped his hat to the tall man and turned away. He walked towards the back door and without a final glance, stepped out into the night.

The tall man looked at the couple. His face was void of emotion. Tanya choked out a "Thank you" as she stared at him. Stephen noticed the man nod slightly and fade away. When they were alone, Tanya kissed Stephen, who smiled and passed out from the pain.

*

Two days later

Stephen stared at the IV tubes in his arms and wondered what pain medication was pumping through his system. Whatever it was, it was amazing.

Tanya, cleaned and refreshed, sat next to his bed. Stephen smiled at his wife. She leaned in and kissed him. He groaned as she wiped the lipstick off his lips. As she pulled away, they were surprised to see a man wearing a grey suit and a fedora standing at the foot of the bed.

"Sorry to disturb you, Mr. and Mrs. Carter. My name is Michael, and I represent a group you may be interested in." He pulled out a card and handed it to Tanya.

She showed the card to Stephen. It was black with gold lettering: 'Michael. Order of Angeliers'.

"Angeliers?" Stephen asked.

"People who can control Arc Angels. Our motto is 'We are the Light against the Darkness'," Michael answered. After a pause he continued with a sorrowful look. "I am sorry for what happened to you. You were on our radar, but they got to you first."

"I don't understand," Tanya said. "How am I able to control these things?"

Michael smiled. "All in good time, Mrs. O'Hare, but first," Michael snapped his fingers. Tanya and Stephen gasped as two Arc Angels appeared by the bed. Pulling a sheaf of papers out of a briefcase, Michael asked, "How would you like join our little organization?"

Renting the Dead

Joe Morris stood next to the road and watched the shabbily dressed woman poke around some bushes in front of an historic white house. He glanced at his watch for the fourth time in ten minutes. It read two-thirty in the morning.

"Hold on a second, I might be on to something," the old woman said as she pulled herself out of the bush.

"I've been holding on for a couple of hours now," Joe said. He shook his head as he watched her. When she walked around the corner, Joe sighed and followed her. As he turned the corner, he saw her backend sticking out of another bush. He hung his head.

It had been two weeks since Joe opened his new restaurant down by the waterfront. The historic town by the water hadn't seen much change since the War of 1812, and he was trying to drag some of it into the twenty-first century. While it had its modern features, Joe had managed to keep the historic front of the building intact, replacing the parts that were beyond repair. The opening night had been a success, but his life would take a strange twist when he opened the next morning.

The old woman was sitting on a chair on his patio when he arrived at eight. She was dressed in a worn grey dress, a felt hat, and long black boots with high heels. Her long straggly grey hair struggled out from under her hat and lay on her shoulders. A large wool bag sat at her feet. Her rose-coloured glasses sat on the mid-point of her nose, just down from her steel blue eyes. To Joe, she looked like a cross between Professor Trelawney and Stevie Nicks.

"You've done quite a nice job with this place. Managed to keep its historic look."

"Kept the Historical Society off my back," Joe said, as he walked by her and took his keys out of his pocket. The old woman gazed across the water at the old castle. When Joe had unlocked the door, she stood up and followed him inside.

"Excuse me, but we're not open for another three hours," Joe said. "I'm sorry but you will have to wait outside."

"Oh, I'm not here to eat. I am here to help you," the old woman said, handing Joe a light purple card. It read:

Genève Roebottom

Conductor of Séances

Spirit Hunter, Exorcist, Parapsychologist,

Spiritual Agent, Car Detailer, and Sous Chef.

Also available for light housekeeping.

No need to contact, will arrive when needed.

"Parapsychologist?" Joe asked.

"Hey, even the dead have problems," Genève answered. "Now, I am not here to analyze some poltergeist who had Daddy issues, or if their mom was sleeping with half the regiment; I am here to give your place some *character*."

"Character? I think I've done a pretty good job of giving this place some character."

"Sir, if I may," Genève said. "Your place looks great and fits in nicely with the historic scenery; however, it lacks something. It needs a ghost."

"A ghost?" Joe bent over laughing and slammed his hand on the nearest table. Genève stood silently, holding her bag and smiling. When Joe recovered, he said, "Lady, that's a good one. I haven't laughed that hard in a long time. Here's your card and have a nice day."

"You know that restaurant just off the main road? It has a ghost and does great business."

Joe stopped laughing and looked at her.

"The old B and B up by golf course has a ghost who slams doors at night. They have a ninety-five percent occupancy all year round."

"Yes, but—" Joe tried to interrupt.

"The old fort has a ton of ghosts. The ghost walking tours make a killing."

"But ghosts aren't real."

"Really? Think about this, Mr. Morris. You had a good opening night because you're new. In about a week, you will see your customers taper off and head back to these other businesses. Why? Because not only do they have historic connections, but their ghosts are also part of their charm. Gives them character."

Joe was silent as Genève turned and walked out the door. He glanced down at the card.

"Good luck Mr. Morris," she said, as she closed the door and walked away.

Joe watched her go and snorted. He threw the card in the garbage and walked to his office.

*

After a solid first week, Joe noticed that the number of customers was dropping off. By the end of the second week, there was hardly anyone in the restaurant. He tried looking for Genève's card, but the garbage had already been cleared.

Depressed, he walked through the dining area and came upon an older couple having their lunch. The wife, a plump lady with streaks of grey hair, sat across from her equally plump husband with no hair. She addressed Joe as he passed.

"What's with the frown?"

Joe looked at the woman, who was pulling on a wool sweater with three Canada geese on the front. He glanced at the husband, who was wearing a similar sweater, with three moose across his. Sighing, he explained the whole affair of dwindling customers and his encounter with Genève.

"Well, I don't know about getting a ghost, but that B and B you mentioned? We stayed there the other night, and I saw the door-banging ghost."

"Really?" Joe asked in a mocking tone.

"Yes, sir, I did," the wife continued, not noticing Joe's tone. "He was in full regimental uniform with his rifle, and stood at the end of the bed, watching us."

"Watching you?" Joe asked.

"Well, to be honest, I didn't mind him being there, you know, because I felt he was protecting us but…" the wife paused before continuing. "He was watching us while we were, you know, having some naughty fun."

Her husband grunted as he forced his eyes down at his half-eaten hamburger, trying desperately to pick up French fries with his fork. Joe stared at the woman. He felt the weight of his situation pushing down on his shoulders. He nodded at the woman, muttered, 'Have a nice day," and walked back to his office.

He was sitting in the office trying to come up with a new promotion when one of his waitresses came in holding a light purple card. He ran into the restaurant and saw Genève standing at the front door. She was smiling.

"Ready?"

Joe glanced at the empty tables and nodded.

*

"Ah, here she is," Genève said, as she pulled herself out of the bushes. She was wearing a leather hat which covered her entire head. Attached to the hat and sitting in front of eyes were the weirdest spectacles he had ever seen. The left lens protruded out about four inches, while the right one was a series of monocles of different strengths.

"I knew she was around here. Mr. Morris, please meet Christina."

Joe was staggered, as a beautiful young woman stepped out from the bush. She had long brown hair and wore a flowing white dress. Her youthful face betrayed a sadness, but she gave Joe a slight smile.

"What was she doing in a bush?" Joe asked.

Genève shrugged. "Who knows why the dead do anything. She most likely hid there when she was a child. It was probably her safe space."

Genève whispered to Christina and led her towards Joe. She tied a small string bracelet with a charm around his wrist and smiled at Christina.

"There, she's yours now. When you get back to the restaurant, put this charm in a safe place, and Christina will stay on the premises."

"OK, but how do I pay her?" Joe asked.

"You don't pay her, you pay me. The dead don't need money. They don't have a debit card or know how to use a bank machine," Genève answered rolling her eyes. "Your payment to her is purpose. The dead lose theirs when they die. Some move on to whatever, but those who linger behind just wander until they find a purpose."

"Like the door banger?" Joe asked.

"Exactly," Genève answered. "You're giving her a purpose, so she should be happy. Me, on the other hand—you owe me five hundred a month."

"Five hundred?" Joe choked and pounded his chest.

"Yes, five hundred," Genève said. "You see, I can help you rent the dead, but if you fail to pay me, I can also repossess them."

"What if you don't know where the charm is?"

"I will know," Genève answered and Joe read her eyes. He believed her. He took out his chequebook and paid her. When she took the cheque, she thanked Joe and spoke:

"Now, you lead Christina back to your restaurant and she will find her place. All will be good."

Joe nodded and walked back to the building. Christina following him. She floated just above the pavement and one step behind him. As they passed under some of the streetlights, Christina seemed to fade then re-appear.

When they reached the restaurant, Christina stopped and looked at the building. Her eyes widened and she floated up and down the street staring at it. Joe thought at first she was looking at the strange configuration, but somewhere in the back of his mind, he realized that she was remembering something from her past.

He gave her a few moments, then opened the door. He walked in and stared out the main window at her. Christina floated, and with a sad smile, passed through the window and into the dining area. Looking around, she found a seat at the back and occupied it.

Joe watched her for a minute longer, then headed to his office. He placed the charm in his safe and returned to see Christina in the same place. He paused for a moment before walking out the front door and locking it. He chuckled for a second when he thought how useless it would be to lock a ghost inside his building. He gave a last glance at Christina before heading home.

*

Business started to boom for the restaurant once word got out. A ghost who sits at the window. People stood in front of the window and took pictures. Patrons requested to sit with her as they ate and, outside of the odd kid throwing things at Christina to see if they passed through her, most people were well-behaved and respectful.

Throughout the boom however, Joe couldn't help but notice that Christina was unhappy. She never moved from her seat and continued to gaze out the window. The only occurrence that brought a smile to her face was when the horse-drawn carriages traveled by.

After a while, the complaints started. "She just sits there," one customer said. "I've tried all the tricks, and she still won't go out with me," said another. It was obvious to Joe that the latter didn't realize that Christina was dead.

One day, as the lunch rush was winding down, Joe noticed Christina looking at him, her eyes pleading. He walked to her booth and sat down across from her. Their eyes met and for the first time since meeting her, Joe noticed her absolute beauty. He had been so busy that he'd ignored her, treating her like part of the furniture. For the first time, Joe wondered if Christina had feelings or a longing for something.

That look haunted Joe as he went to bed that night. She hung around the edge of his consciousness. He slept badly. In the middle of the night, he arose to wash his face and shake the awkward dreams away. As he returned to bed, he glanced out his window to see a man walking a horse through the streets. Joe got the impression that this man was looking for something or someone. He watched for a moment before returning to bed.

Towards morning, Joe dreamed of leading a horse along the streets, checking bushes and behind trees. At one point, he turned to the horse and asked, "What am I looking for?"

With a sarcastic tone, the horse answered, "How do I know? It's your dream."

*

Instead of heading to the restaurant the following morning, Joe went to see Genève. Her house was located at the far end of the town in a small, wooded area. Tall hedges lined the front yard, with a rusty iron gate in the middle. When Joe opened it, it gave a high squeal that hurt his ears.

The old house stared at him as he walked towards the concrete steps. Somewhere in his heart, Joe could feel the welcoming façade slip away and reveal its fierce solitude, a hiding place for spirits and the restless dead. He found himself unable to lift his right foot onto the first step. His breathing was tight, and beads of sweat appeared on his forehead.

The sound of a vacuum broke the spell, and Joe turned towards the side of the house. He shook the uneasiness from his shoulders and walked towards the sound, which led him around the corner of the house to an old Plymouth Duster. Its passenger door was open, and a yellow coverall-covered butt was sticking out. He was about to speak when the vacuum stopped and

Genève emerged from the car, a Dust Buster in one hand and a chocolate bar in the other.

"Hi," she said as she chewed her bar. "I was wondering when you were going to show up?"

"You actually detail cars?" Joe asked.

"Well, you don't think I get by on your five hundred a month, do you?" she replied, finishing her bar and wiping her hand on her coveralls. "So, she just sits by the window, eh?"

"You could feel that through your so-called powers?" Joe asked.

Genève laughed out loud. "No, you fool, it's all over town. Come on in." She waved her hand and led him into the back door of the house.

The smell of incense hit him the second he was inside. The narrow hallway was framed with pictures of strange creatures and misty castles in the mountains. As they walked through the dust in the living room, Joe couldn't shake the feeling of being watched, although no one else was in the house.

Genève's cramped office was filled with old books and parchments. Shrunken heads hung from gold chains tacked to the wall, their eyes shooting through him. Half-burned black candles and their holders filled the sill of the only window in the room. Their shadows looked like prison bars.

"Ah, here she is," Genève said, opening an old leather-bound book. Blowing away some dust, she read from a passage: "Christina Blake, third wife to Thomas Blake. Oh, I remember him—he was a right bastard."

"Remember him?" Joe asked.

"From the book." Genève smiled as she continued reading. "His first two wives died under mysterious circumstances. Christina endured terrible beatings and hid in the bushes when Thomas came home from the inns. A horrible drunk he was."

"So that's how you found her. Her ghost was hiding in the bushes."

Genève touched her nose and carried on. "She had an affair with a coach driver; Simms was his name. They would meet in his barn and make love in the hay." Scrunching her nose, she continued, "Hope the hay was clean. Well, old Thomas found out and hunted them down. He killed them in cold blood in the barn, but was seen by the stable boy, whose father served in the local regiment. Thomas was captured, tried, and hung for his crimes."

Joe shook his head. "What a story." He told her about his dream, about leading a horse and carriage. Genève smiled.

"He's still looking for her—Simms that is. Blake too. Goodness, I hate triangles."

"Love triangles?" Joe asked.

"Yes, three points, three people, no movement. It doesn't move; in fact, it just sits there," she answered.

"But a triangle is stable, isn't it?" Joe asked.

"True, but you can't put anything on it like you can with a square. A triangle is useless. It's only good for one thing and that's holding things down. Like love."

Joe paused for a moment but before he could say anything Genève said, "Look at the time. I must finish that car and get over to the Lakeside Tavern. Girl's got to work."

Before Joe realized what was happening, Genève had escorted him out of the house and back to his car.

"Look for Simms. He is the key to finding Christina's smile and purpose."

"I thought my restaurant was her purpose," Joe said.

"Come on. Do you really think that's her real purpose?" With the question hanging in the air, Genève disappeared behind the house.

Joe stood dumbfounded by his car. It seemed to take forever for him to find his car keys and leave.

*

After another day of customers bitching at him for Christina's lack of movement or emotion, Joe decided to take the bracelet charm out of the safe and lead Christina out into the street. It was after midnight when they left the restaurant. She followed him as he walked aimlessly through the town.

"Simms. Where do you think he is?" Joe asked her. At hearing his name, Christina smiled and became animated. She glided up the road, close to the old regiment barn. Joe ran to keep up with her. He followed her through the open gates. Christina glided up and down the stalls. looking in each. Undaunted, she left the barn and continued to search the streets. At the crossroads of the main junction, Joe spotted a ghostly figure leading a team of horses and a carriage. Christina stopped and gazed at the figure.

The figure, a young man in full regimental dress, looked up and smiled. Joe assumed that this was Simms. Christina floated towards the young man, who embraced her. Joe smiled at the reunion. As he looked down at the charm in his hand, Joe felt the air turn cold. Feeling a presence, Joe turned to see the apparition of a bearded man with a large knife in his hand. A noose hung loosely from his neck.

Before Joe could move, the apparition thrust the knife into his chest. Joe closed his eyes and waited for the pain. Nothing happened. He opened his eyes to see the confused look on the apparition's face. It thrust the knife into Joe's chest again. Joe laughed.

"Thomas Blake, you really are a thunderhead. You can't kill me, stupid sod."

Blake smiled and walked past Joe. Joe turned and saw Blake head towards the ghostly lovers.

"Christina! Simms! It's Blake!" he shouted.

Christina pulled away from Simms' embrace and floated away up the street. Simms stood his ground for a moment, then turned as if he heard something. Joe could see Christina opening her mouth. It was some sort of afterlife yell.

Simms nodded and jumped into the carriage. As Blake approached, Simms flicked the reins, and the horses took off. They shot by Blake and up the other street. Joe watched them go. When Simms was gone, Joe realized that Blake staring at him. He also noticed that Christina was gone as well.

Blake stared at Joe for a few more moments before walking down a side street and disappearing. Joe stood in the middle of the road as the rain started, glistening the road with the reflection of the flashing yellow light.

*

He found Christina a little while later in the bushes, the same ones that Genève had found her in. Joe could see her clutching her knees to her chest and rocking back and forth. He tried to talk to her but found no words.

"Looking for the words?" a voice called out to him.

Joe glanced back to see Genève walking towards him. He nodded. "What do you say to a ghost?"

"Anything you want. It's up to them whether they acknowledge you or not." She looked in the bushes and shook her head. "Bloody Blake."

"He stabbed me earlier," Joe said, regaling her with the encounter from earlier.

"You're lucky," Genève said.

"Did the charm protect me?" Joe asked.

Genève laughed out loud. "No, you fool. Ghosts can't physically hurt anybody. Most people just die of shock. Now, poltergeists, they're the real bastards. *They* can kill you."

"The charm?" Joe asked.

"Not now, later," she spoke.

"If Blake can't hurt me, can he hurt Christina?"

"Yes and no," Genève answered, while looking at the young girl. "Physically no, but he can torture her mentally for eternity. And if he gets hold of her, it will be tough to get her back."

"What can we do?"

Genève straightened up and looked at him, her blue eyes staring through him. After a moment she sighed and spoke, "OK, follow me."

*

Half an hour later, Joe was standing in Genève's living room, staring a ghost who was sitting in an armchair, staring straight ahead and not moving. Genève called out from the back.

"That's Sitting Steve. He just sits there at night. No reason."

Joe stared at Steve for a moment before joining Genève at the back. She was in a large walk-in closet rifling through an old trunk.

"What are you looking for, a proton pack?"

He laughed out loud, but stopped when he noticed her glare.

"Do I look like Dan fucking Aykroyd to you?"

Joe shook his head. Genève continued her search. A minute later, she pulled a small object out and looked at it. Nodding, she walked by Joe and motioned for him to follow. As they walked out of the living room, he said, "See ya, Steve."

Steve blinked, raised his hand and waved.

*

It was an hour later when Joe and Genève walked along the streets. Joe had enquired about the object she carried, but she rebuffed him. They wandered the streets until they came to the bush where Christina still hid.

Genève coaxed her out using kind words and the promise to keep her safe. Joe kept glancing around, searching for both Simms and Blake. Though he felt no physical danger, he feared for Christina and Simms, and what Blake could do to them.

As they walked the streets, Christina suddenly lit up and turned down a side street. Joe and Genève followed. The street led to a small barn. At the door, holding his spectral horses, stood Simms. His face brightened at the sight of Christina.

She floated to him, and the two ghosts embraced. Joe felt happy about the reunion. He was about to pull the charm from his pocket when Genève stayed his hand.

"Look, up the alley."

Joe turned to see Blake. He was dressed as before and still holding the large knife. Simms and Christina had also seen the menace. Simms pulled himself away from Christina and strode past Joe and Genève towards Blake. Christina opened her mouth to scream but nothing came out.

Joe followed Simms and they walked towards Blake. Before he could get three steps, Genève grabbed him by the jacket. He shook her hand off and followed the young man.

As he walked along in step with the ghost, Simms gave Joe a sideways glance and a smile. He was glad to have someone to back him up. Blake raised his knife and ran towards the two men. Simms drew a large sword from his scabbard and braced himself for the attack.

Joe stood by helplessly, knowing he couldn't interfere. The two ghosts engaged in a spectral battle. After parrying with each other, Blake made a move and thrust his knife into Simms. Christina screamed again, and Joe gaped at the scene.

Simms fell to his knees as Blake walked by without waiting for him to fully collapse. Marching towards Christina, he grabbed the young lady by the hair. Before he could stab her, Blake turned to yell at Simms. He was astonished to see Simms stand up and walk towards them. Blake let go of Christina and brandished his knife again.

Before they engaged, Genève yelled out, "Enough! Thomas Blake, I banish you from this realm!" She held the object in front of Blake. Blake froze. Christina floated to Simms; they embraced.

Blake stared at the object and started to glow. He lifted his hands and reached out to the young lovers. With a silent scream, Blake disappeared in a flash of light.

Joe stared at the scene. He looked at Genève and pointed to the object.

"It's just a ring made of Labradorite. Special qualities?"

"No, but to deal with the dead and make suggestions, they need something in the real world to focus on. The object doesn't matter, just the suggestion."

Joe turned towards Christina and Simms. Happy with their reunion, he slowly pulled out the charm and handed it

Genève. He nodded to the three of them and turned away. As he walked out of the alley, it started to rain.

"Perfect," Joe said, as he walked towards the restaurant.

*

Two weeks later, Genève walked into the restaurant and saw Joe talking to some of the patrons. She waited patiently until he noticed her and came over.

"How's business?" she asked, as three waitresses scurried by.

"Excellent. It turns out that I had a companion on the way home two weeks ago."

Genève looked past Joe to see the apparition of an old Newfoundland dog walking around the restaurant. He would pause at different tables, letting little kids give him food only to have the morsels fall to the floor. Genève smiled.

"After he was here for a couple of days, I found a dog biscuit in the pocket of my jacket. I don't own any dogs, so how'd it end up there?"

He paused and reached into his pocket. He pulled out a cheque and with a smile, handed it to Genève. She quietly accepted it and put it in her purse. They regarded each other for a moment before Genève turned and headed for the door.

"Give my best to Steve."

Genève turned, waved, and headed out into the street.

A Changing of the Guard

Iceland, 2170

"Death certainly is eternal, and I should know. I've been dead for a very long time."

The vampire looked down at her former companion. Kristos, the tall Grecian who looked after her every whim, lay on a stone slab. Beside her was Inga, Kristos' replacement. She was also tall, and blond as the man on the stone. The vampire smiled inside. He knew what she liked.

"How long was he your companion?" Inga asked.

The vampire paused before answering.

"Over three hundred years." She touched his beautiful but hard face. "He stepped off a boat just outside New Orleans. Walked across the town until he found the tailor shop down a forgotten alley."

"Tailor shop?"

"Yes. You see, we creatures that stalk our prey are not animals. We dress in only the best clothes. This shop catered to the unusual, and supplied hard-to-get wear."

The vampire paused again. "In the back of the shop was a small speakeasy. I was there with my friend and fellow blood drinker, Romero, when this fine specimen walked in. He walked right up to me and presented me with a parchment. An offer of employment."

Inga remained silent as the vampire gazed upon her companion. She could see the vampire struggling with tears.

"It was a reference from an acquaintance from Europe. I looked up from the parchment and agreed immediately."

New Orleans, 1820

"Of course you will have to have a formal interview," Cassandra said, as she led Kristos out of the speakeasy and into the alley. They flagged down a horse and carriage, and an hour later, they disembarked at a large estate. She led him into the house and straight to her bedroom.

"Is this where the interview is to take place?" he asked.

Cassandra dropped her dress, ripped off her corset, and lay naked on the bed. She smiled at the young man standing in front of her.

"Fool, you already have the job. Impress me with your disrobing."

Kristos smiled and slowly undressed, Cassandra's eyes yearning. When he was naked, she motioned to him. He climbed on the bed, his eyes bewitched by her beauty. Soon, he was in her arms and in her. Their lovemaking was animalistic. When they climaxed, she bit into his neck, increasing their pleasure.

In the afterglow he asked, "Have you turned me?"

"No," she answered. "I just marked you. You're mine."

"For the rest of my life?"

Iceland, 2170

"For the rest of your life," Cassandra said, as she touched his chest. Her cold vampire heart cracked as she spoke.

"You loved him," Inga said.

Cassandra nodded slightly. She closed her eyes and willed the tears to come, but they did not. The pair stood in silence as the Icelandic fires raged beneath them. It was the perfect place to send him into the afterlife. After a moment, Inga asked, "What did he do for you?"

New Orleans, 1840

The masked ball was in full swing as Kristos navigated his way through the crowd. Cassandra had taught him to be patient, to seek out the perfect victim—someone who wouldn't be missed, even by high society.

He found the young woman in a corner by herself. He recognized her as the daughter of one of the minor families in Louisiana. Within a minute, he'd seduced her and offered her a dance. The young lady felt she was in a dream as the other dancers gazed at her and this handsome stranger.

When the dance was over, Kristos led the young woman to a waiting carriage down the road from the hall. When they arrived at the estate, Kristos brought the young woman to the bedroom, where she was shocked to see a naked Cassandra stalking towards her. Cassandra bewitched the young woman who, under her spell, allowed the vampire and Kristos to have their fun.

In the morning, Kristos took the unconscious young woman to edge of the swamp where he was met by a loathsome creature. Payment was made, and the young woman was brought to a place on the outskirts of New Orleans. She would be found several hours later with no memory of the night before.

Iceland, 2170

"Usually, I would have killed the victim, but Kristos wouldn't hear of it. It was one of the few matters I allowed him to counsel me on," Cassandra said, smiling to herself. "They were amazing times."

Inga stayed silent. After a few moments Cassandra asked, "How did he find you?"

Inga stared at Kristos.

"I don't know. He just did."

Sweden, 2170

Inga stepped out of her house and wandered down to the shore. As she gathered water from the sea, she saw one of the new airships sail over her small village. It landed in the large field, and many of the villagers ran to it. As the crew dropped off mail and other supplies, Inga noticed a tall man exit the ship. He briefly looked around, and noticed her.

To Inga's shock, the man began to walk in her direction. She turned and ran to her small hut, racing inside and shutting the door. She sat at her small table in silence. Suddenly she heard the crunching of boots outside. A knock on the door soon followed.

"Miss Inga Berg, I know you are in there. My name is Kristos, and I have a job offer for you."

Inga slowly went to the door. She opened it to see the tall man smiling back at her. He was handsome and disarming. After an awkward moment, she asked him in and offered him some cold tea. He accepted.

"What kind of job offer?" she asked.

"Well, you see, I am about to leave my employer, and she needs a replacement. You seem perfect."

"How did you find me?"

"I have a gift for finding people who will satisfy my employer. I stood on the tarmac in Iceland and picked this airship. When we arrived here, I stepped off, spotted you, and here we are."

"That's quite a gift, but how do you know you I am perfect for the job? I could be happy here."

Kristos looked around the small hut.

"Happy?" he asked. "Let me see: family gone, destitute, barely scraping a living together doing laundry and other menial chores. You're alone despite your good looks, because there isn't anyone around here worth loving. If you were to marry someone, you would be a prisoner in a loveless marriage."

"Who says I won't be prisoner with your employer?" Inga asked.

"Good question," he answered. "However, take my word for it. I've worked for her for a *long* time, and I have never felt like a prisoner." Kristos took out a small parchment and handed it to her. "Now, I must be on that airship. I expect you in a month."

Inga was about to protest when Kristos stood up. He gave her a small peck on the cheek and left the hut. After he was gone, Inga unfolded the parchment. It contained enough money for passage to Iceland, and elaborated on the duties the job entailed. Reading them she was intrigued.

Iceland, 2170

"I never thought leaving your employment involved killing himself," Inga said to Cassandra.

"He didn't kill himself. He just allowed himself to die."

Inga stared at Cassandra. The vampire gestured towards a large glass decanter sitting on a small table. It was a mixture of blue and red liquid that flowed around each other.

"The elixir of life," Cassandra said. "It was my friend Victor who discovered it. He replicated it in his laboratory just before Kristos came to me. One glass a month led to a lifetime of adventures."

"Or servitude," Inga said.

"Kristos was never my slave," Cassandra countered. "He was my companion, lover, confidant. He ran the household with discipline and kindness. My staff loved him."

"Why stop taking the elixir?"

"He said he was tired of life. He had lived many lifetimes and was ready for the afterlife."

Inga stared down at Kristos. He looked peaceful.

"He didn't look tired to me," Inga said.

"He always put on a brave face. He never let anyone aside from me know his true emotions."

Cassandra bent down and kissed her companion one last time before straightening and pulling a small lever. The stone slab tilted up, and Kristo slid down the ramp and into the fires below the mountain. The two women stood in silence for a moment. Cassandra pulled the lever a second time, and the slab returned to its original position. Turning to Inga, she said, "Now, it is time to interview you properly."

Cassandra took Inga by the hand and led her out of the room. They strode up a long ramp that led into the main part of the castle. Inga had been quite taken with the castle, an impressive structure carved out of the mountain by ancient hands, when she'd arrived. Kristos had familiarized her with the place, but not every nook and cranny.

Ingo pulled her coat close around her neck. Despite the mountain fires, there was still a chill hanging from the rock. Cassandra was wrapped in a long fur coat. When Inga asked why she wore the garment, the vampire answered, "At my age, even my vampiric tolerance to heat and cold has started to fail. A thousand years of living will do that."

At the top of the ramp, Cassandra pulled Inga down a small hallway which led to a large bedroom with a roaring fire. A four-poster bed was the centrepiece. On a small table to the left of the fireplace was a decanter like the one in the first room. Beside it was a small glass. Inga glanced at the vampire, who nodded while she stripped off her clothes.

As Inga poured the liquid into the glass, Cassandra stared her new companion, and felt a warmth build in her insides. As she put the glass to her lips, Inga asked, "Why did you move to Iceland?"

Cassandra smiled and lay back on the bed.

"Think of the world as a slightly bent coin. We, the monsters, occupy the concave side, with the ordinary people on the other. There are those out there that walk along the side of the coin. The hunters."

"Have you been hunted?"

"Yes," Cassandra paused. "It all started with a young woman named Sarah MacDaniel. She and her brother Hugo killed Victor and used the elixir for themselves. We've had many battles with them…but I am sure the archives will answer all your questions. Kristos was quite the chronicler."

Inga paused as she put the glass to her lips. She glanced at Cassandra, whose dark eyes called to her. "I don't know if I can measure up."

"Drink, you fool. You already have the job."

Inga drank deeply. The liquid burned her throat, but she felt elation rise from within. The next thing Inga knew, she was naked and in bed with her new employer. Inga's heightened senses gave her amazing pleasure, and soon she was marked.

In the afterglow, she asked, "Will we be hunted?"

"Yes, but tonight, you're my only bounty," Cassandra answered, and kissed her new companion.

*

Two days later, a large ship entered the Icelandic capital. As it disgorged its supplies, two figures walked down the gangway. Once on the pier, the tall bald man and his female assistant took stock of the city. He smelled the air.

"She's here."

"Are you sure, Master Hugo?"

Hugo Macdaniel smiled, picked up his bag and led his assistant into the city.

The Whisperers

"**J**immie! They took her!" Janie shouted at her twin brother.

"Who…took who?" Jimmie asked, as he rolled over in bed, still half-asleep.

"Ted Brewster and that fink Donnie Allister. They grabbed Suzie from our front door."

Jimmie got up and ran to the window. Ted Brewster's black van was pulling away from the curb. He turned to Janie and nodded. They quickly dressed and ran downstairs. Two minutes later, dressed in winter boots, parkas, hats, and gloves, the twins ran out of the house in search of their babysitter.

*

Suzie Thomas was still trying to fathom what had happened to her. One minute she was babysitting her favourite twins, the next she was bound and gagged in the back of a van. She shook her head and ran the events through her mind.

After a supper of pizza and gooey treats, the three of them had watched a couple of cheesy horror movies. Teeth brushed, kisses, and promises of pancakes in the morning, the kids went to bed without a fuss. Suzie was just channel surfing when a knock on the door revealed Ted Brewster, the quarterback of Thorsson High's football team, the Hammers.

Suzie, an average-looking eighteen-year-old with her brown hair constantly in a ponytail, was a little surprised to see him at the door.

"Hi Suzie. Can I talk to you outside for a moment?" Ted asked, standing in the snow. dressed in jeans, a hoody, and a black jacket with the crossed hammer crest.

Suzie quickly put on her boots and parka and stepped outside. Ted smiled and motioned her towards his van. As she stepped away from the house, the van door opened to reveal Donnie Allister, a greasy-looking idiot who had been kicked out of school for fighting.

Before Suzie could react, Ted grabbed her from behind. Donnie slapped a piece of duct tape over her lips and quickly pulled her into the van. Suzie got an arm free and managed a quick punch to Donnie's neck which sent him flying backwards, clutching his throat.

Ted grabbed her hands and forced her down on the floor of the van. He quickly tied her hands and feet. Suzie screamed through the tape, but Ted laughed at her. Turning to Donnie he said, "Nice going, tough guy."

Donnie, still coughing from the punch, threw Ted a middle finger. Satisfied that Suzie was secure, Ted got into the front seat and turned on the ignition. As he pulled away from the curb, he shouted to Donnie to look after Suzie.

Donnie grunted and stared at Suzie, who matched his gaze.

"I've never liked you, Suzie Thomas, and I'm going to enjoy watching what happens to you."

Suzie continued to stare at Donnie until he pulled her hood over her head and turned her over on her stomach. As she struggled against her bonds, Suzie tried to organize her thoughts.

"What the hell was going on?"

*

Constable Gerry O'Brien pulled out of the Tim Horton's drive thru, sipping his coffee and efficiently navigating the slippery road at the same time. He knew he was perpetuating the stereotype of cops and doughnut shops, but he didn't care. Gerry knew the folks of Otherville didn't think of him that way, seeing as he was six-foot-four and very fit.

As he pulled off Main Street and towards the affluent side of town, he spotted the McKracken twins running down their street. A quick glance at the radio informed him of the late hour of eleven thirty. Gerry pulled his cruiser over to the sidewalk and rolled along at a slow speed to match the twins. He lowered the window and spoke to the kids.

"Hey, what are you two doing out here at this hour?"

The twins turned towards Gerry.

"We're looking for Suzie Thomas," Janie answered.

"She was looking after us for the weekend," Jimmie said.

"Mom and Dad are in Toronto for a conference," Janie said.

"Suzie stepped outside to talk to Ted Brewster and—" Jimmie said.

"—He and that stupid jerk Donnie Allister kidnapped her," Janie finished.

Gerry found himself whipping his head back and forth like watching a tennis match. He threw his car into Park and stepped out onto the sidewalk. He put up his hands and asked them to stop speaking. Taking a deep breath, he asked Janie to repeat the story. When she finished Gerry asked, "Are you sure it was a kidnapping or just harmless fun?"

The twins looked at each other. After a moment Janie said, "They forced her into the van, Constable Gerry. Donnie put tape on her mouth."

"She also punched Donnie in the throat. She wasn't playing," Jimmie added.

Gerry looked at the twins. He didn't see anything that indicated their story was a prank.

"Get in," he said, pointing to the cruiser. The twins ran to the car and climbed into the back.

Gerry got behind the wheel and picked up his radio handset. He called the incident in, along with a description of Ted's van. He pulled away from the curb and headed back along Main Street.

*

Elias Talbot, the Mayor of Otherville, stood just within the tree line of Barn Owl Hollow. A skinny man with thinning hair, Talbot was freezing, even though he wore many layers of clothing. Beside him was the reason for him being there: Barry Sanders—a small mousey man with a bad moustache and sneaky eyes. His breath hung in the air as he spoke. "Cold night, eh Mayor?"

Talbot rolled his eyes. He hated Sanders. The man was a snake who made shady deals and was rumoured to have screwed over some of the best businessmen in Otherville. If there was a buck to be made, Sanders made it off someone else's misery.

"You know this isn't going to work," Talbot said to Sanders. "You're just taking advantage of their grief."

"It's the old woman who is taking advantage of their grief; I'm just facilitating the arrangement."

"You mean taking a finder's fee for a crackpot. Is there any level of deception you won't lower yourself to?"

Sanders was about to speak when a red minivan pulled up to the hollow. Two men jumped out and opened the side door. A small woman in a wheelchair was taken out and carried over to Talbot and Sanders. Talbot thought the woman looked ancient. Sanders spoke to the woman.

"Ah, Miss Crawford, thank you for coming. This is Mayor Talbot."

Miss Crawford nodded towards Talbot. Behind her were two of the meanest men Talbot had ever seen. Both were over six feet, and wide across the shoulders. Their faces seemed to be made of leather. With a small gesture from Miss Crawford, the two men picked up the wheelchair and moved it to the centre of the hollow.

"Where did you find her?" Talbot asked.

"Toronto. She has a shop claiming the usual stuff, palm readings, fortunes, and whatnot. What got me was that she claimed to be a mythical whisperer."

"What?" Talbot asked.

"The ability to talk to mythical creatures."

Talbot turned his head in disgust. "How did you convince the Andersons to agree to this?"

"Vengeance. Their son disappeared here a year ago tonight. The Andersons haven't been the same since."

"I know, but this is cruel, Sanders. I mean, couldn't you let them be in peace?"

"Everyone has emotional buttons, Mayor, I just happen to know which ones to push."

Talbot shook his head. He knew he shouldn't be there, but Harry Anderson was a friend and had asked him personally. He had tried to talk Harry out of it, but his wife Myrtle was adamant. Now, as he stood in the cold, Talbot thought of his friend and the money he'd spent for a hopeless cause.

The sound of engines caught his ear, and soon Talbot witnessed half a dozen cars pull into the hollow, led by Harry Anderson. The last vehicle was a black van.

"Here we go," Sanders said, as he walked over to the Andersons' car. Talbot shuddered.

*

"Sorry Gerry, nothing on this side of town," the voice of Constable Dyson said over the radio.

Gerry acknowledged the transmission and hung up the handset. He glanced in his rear-view mirror at the twins.

"Sorry. It seems the van has disappeared."

The twins said nothing. Gerry pulled out of the empty mall parking lot and back to towards City Hall. As they drove, Gerry noticed Nancy Willis, the executive assistant to Mayor Talbot, walking along Main Street. On a whim, Gerry pulled over. Rolling down his window, he addressed the young woman.

"Hi, Nancy. How's it going?"

Nancy Willis was a small woman with dark auburn hair which was currently concealed within her parka hood. Her snow pants and big boots obscured her curvy figure. She waved to Gerry before answering.

"It's going fine. I have a meeting with the mayor, budget stuff."

"On a Saturday night at this hour?" Gerry asked.

"Couldn't wait. I was to meet him at City Hall after he returned from some emergency meeting."

"He didn't invite you along?" Gerry asked.

"No. He said the less I knew, the better."

Gerry nodded and felt a tap on the shoulder. Jimmie leaned forward and poked his head into the front so Nancy could see him. Nancy smiled and recognized Jimmie. She also noticed Janie in the back of the cruiser. Jimmie waved and asked, "Where did the mayor go?"

"Barn Owl Hollow, just down the highway," Nancy replied. "Strange place for a meeting. Why are you kids with Gerry?"

Gerry explained the disappearance of Suzie Thomas in Ted Brewster's van.

"Really? Funny about that—I saw a black van head out towards the hollow about half an hour ago."

"Right. Thanks Nancy, you have been a great help," Gerry said.

"Hope you find her," Nancy replied, as the cruiser pulled away from the curb, the twins waving at her from the back window.

*

Mayor Talbot stared at the Andersons as they consulted with Miss Crawford. Harry was a former football player and athlete. Myrtle was tall like her husband, and a recognized beauty. However, they both looked like shells of themselves. Talbot shook his head.

He noticed Sanders talking to Ted Brewster beside a black van. Sanders handed the young quarterback an envelope, which he put in his pocket. Behind them, Miss Crawford's henchmen were taking a large package out of the minivan. They brought it to the centre of the hollow and opened it. A huge pile of raw meat spilled out onto the snow.

What the hell is going on? Talbot thought.

More people arrived. It was mostly relatives of the Andersons, along with two local hunters, John Bishop and

Craig Parsons. They both wore white camouflage hunting outfits with their rifles slung over their shoulders.

This is going to end badly, Talbot thought, as he watched Miss Crawford motion to Sanders. Sanders nodded to Brewster who opened the van door. Talbot watched in horror as they pulled Suzie Thomas out of the van and dragged her towards the meat.

*

"Tyler Anderson," Gerry said, as he drove towards the hollow. "He was a young football player who, on a dare, walked out into the hollow with a hunting knife and a small camping stove to stay the night."

"Why?" Janie asked.

"It's a hazing ritual for the football team. The idea is that the player must hunt like an owl, hence Barn Owl Hollow, and cook his meal before dawn."

"Sounds stupid," Jimmie said.

"It is stupid," Gerry continued. "Anyway, when the team came back a few hours later to check on him, all they found were ripped clothes, small empty containers of food, and a puddle of blood. The only clue was a series of huge footprints leaving the scene."

Silence filled the cruiser. Gerry continued, "By the time we got out there, the footprints were covered in snow, and we lost the trail. We found no trace of Tyler."

"I think our dad did some of the work on the blood," Janie said. "I overheard him talking to mom about it."

"That's right, but it offered no other clues. Tyler's parents were distraught. They were never the same again."

They drove on in silence. As Gerry pulled onto the highway on the outskirts of town, Janie sat up and looked out the window. Her eyes went wide. Jimmie noticed his sister's expression.

"Janie, what's wrong?"

Janie stared out the window for a moment longer, then said to Gerry, "Hurry! It's coming!"

*

Miss Crawford's men held Talbot back as Ted and Donnie lay Suzie in the middle of the Hollow. They tied her more securely and left her.

Talbot screamed, "What in God's name are you doing?"

A hand on the shoulder quieted him. Talbot turned to see Harry Anderson.

"She won't be harmed; it's just a little incentive. We need bait."

"Harry, please, what are you doing?" Talbot asked.

"This is for Tyler," Harry said. To the hunters he yelled. "Bishop, Parsons, go in and flush it out."

*

Suzie struggled on the snow but couldn't move. She cursed Ted and Donnie, and promised herself that they would pay for this. She turned at the sound of footsteps and watched the two men with rifles walk into the woods. Once they disappeared into the trees, Suzie thought of the twins, and wondered how they were. She hoped they were safe at home in bed.

*

Bishop walked ahead of Parsons with his rifle at the ready. Parsons was laughing.

"This is a joke, Bishop. There is nothing out here."

"Shut up, Parsons," Bishop said, with a laugh. "Anderson is paying for the show, and this is the easiest thousand bucks I have ever earned."

Parsons laughed again, turned towards a tree and unzipped his pants. Relief warmed his insides as he emptied his bladder. He was about to say something rude to Bishop when the tree in front of him moved.

Bishop turned at the scream. He stared at the sight and wet himself. His rifle slipped out of his hand, and terror was the last thing he ever felt.

*

Talbot turned towards the flashing lights of the RCMP cruiser as it pulled into the hollow. Miss Crawford's men walked towards the vehicle as it stopped. Talbot recognized Constable O'Brien as he stepped out and opened the back door. To his surprise, two young teenagers slipped out of the car. The young girl was screaming, "Get out of here! It's coming!"

Talbot rushed towards the group. He noticed that O'Brien had pulled his gun out and was pointing it at Miss Crawford's men.

"Back the hell off!" Gerry yelled at the big men, who slowly raised their hands and took a couple of steps back. When Talbot met the kids, he recognized them.

"What's going on?" he asked Janie.

"That," Janie said, as the screaming started.

*

Suzie shrieked through her gag as the creature stepped into the hollow. It was twenty feet tall with a stag's head. It wore patches of white fur on parts of its body and, though skinny, it had huge muscles on its arms. Blood dripped from its lips, and it carried what was left of Bishop in its right hand. It took a couple of steps and threw Bishop's body into the centre of the hollow.

Miss Crawford motioned to her bodyguards. They ran from Gerry, lifted her wheelchair, and carried her towards the centre of the hollow, placing her twenty feet in front of it.

Miss Crawford started a low chant, which got the creature's attention. It stalked over to her.

"Wendigo," she chanted, and added more words in a language no one understood.

The Andersons stared at the creature with hatred in their eyes. Sanders was drinking from a flask he'd retrieved from his pocket. The twins and Gerry stood next to Talbot, transfixed by the scene. Ted and Donnie had hidden in the van.

As the creature stared at Miss Crawford, one of her bodyguards pulled a small handgun from his pocket. As the creature leaned in close, the guard pointed the gun and fired.

The shot hit the creature in the centre of the chest, and it recoiled. Miss Crawford stopped chanting and smiled.

The creature shook its head and looked down at the hole in its chest. After a couple of deep breaths, the hole shrank and disappeared. Miss Crawford's smile left her face as the creature stepped up and grabbed her wheelchair. The old woman screamed as the creature threw her high above the trees and into the woods.

The two bodyguards froze as the creature turned towards them, then screamed in unison as the creature grabbed them. In one motion, the creature threw the men into treeline.

"So much for the silver bullet," Sanders said, as he took a couple of steps back.

While everyone screeched in terror, the twins ran forward and stood in front of Suzie. The creature stalked over and stopped in front of the kids. Janie had her right hand up, while Jimmie held her left.

"It's OK," she said in a quiet voice. "I can see him in your eyes. Just let him go."

The creature took a step back and grunted.

"Let him go," Janie repeated.

The creature shook and fell to its knees. It convulsed and started to shrink. Moments later, it transformed itself into a young man, while a ghostly fog drifted above him.

"Tyler!" Myrtle tried to race forward but was held back by her husband.

Tyler fell on his side breathing heavily. Janie spoke to the fog.

"Leave this place. There is no need for another host."

The fog hesitated before floating towards the crowd. Talbot watched in horror as the fog passed him and engulfed Sanders, who was backing away. Sanders choked and coughed as the fog entered his mouth. He convulsed and fell to his knees.

The twins released each other and untied Suzie. Once freed, she hugged and kissed them both. Jimmie turned and stared at Sanders. He pulled away from Suzie and ran to him. The sound of ripping clothes filled the air as Sanders grew into a hideous form about ten feet tall. Jimmie spoke to Sanders.

"Just go, and no one will bother you."

Sanders stared at Jimmie and, with an unnatural howl, ran into the woods and disappeared. Jimmie turned around to see the Andersons hugging Tyler, and Gerry knocking on the van door. When Ted and Donnie opened the van, Gerry arrested them for kidnapping.

Suzie and Janie joined Jimmie while Talbot was on his cell phone to Carol Ulster, the head of the Otherville police.

"Chief, better come out to the hollow. Also, get hold of Nancy for me at City Hall. It's going to be a long night."

*

When Dr. John and Dr. Abigail McKracken returned on Sunday, they were not prepared for the story they heard. Suzie told them about Janie and Jimmie's bravery, and recounted the entire incident. The McKrackens were surprised by their children's talents and immediately called the Andersons.

*

Two days later, when Tyler was feeling better, it came out that the football team had placed human skin from the biology lab amongst the food he had to eat for the hazing ritual, which was what had enticed the creature. Tyler said he didn't remember anything after that. All involved were punished, and the bodies of those killed were recovered. Sanders was never found.

*

Later in the week Jimmie and Janie sat in the living room after school, watching tv.

"What do you think happened to Sanders?" Janie asked.

Jimmie stared at the TV and thought for a moment. "I don't know."

Janie nodded and turned back to the show. After a moment she said, "I wonder if we will see him again."

Five days later

Sanders was running through the woods. He was confused and lost. Hunger drove him, and he was desperate. He couldn't catch any prey, and he was weak. He fell and crawled amongst the trees.

A scent caught his nose, and he scrambled to his feet and ran. He found two black bears eating a deer. As he approached, the bears turned on him and scared him away. Sanders moaned and cried out in hunger.

As he sat watching the bears, he felt himself change. The fog floated away from him and left him naked in the woods. Sanders got to his feet, stumbling as he walked, and tried to get his bearings. He didn't know where he was. He saw the glowing lights of a town in the distance and headed towards it.

Sanders had only walked ten feet when he heard the snuffle of a bear behind him. He glanced at the city glow above the trees and asked for mercy. It was a long time coming.

Stranded

Island off the Labrador coast, 1816

"Samuel Brown. You killed me."

Samuel Brown woke up from a dark dream and banged his head on the overturned rowboat he was sleeping under. As he rubbed his head, he heard the rain tapping on the boat. He gave a slight smile and lay back.

"It's raining."

Samuel's back ached as he lay on the rocks. He reached out from under the boat and grabbed the small mug. It was half full of water. He swallowed the sweet rain, then placed the mug back out to collect more. His mind went back to the dream. He could see old Pierce pointing at him.

"You killed me."

"Yes, I did!" Samuel yelled. "Yes, I did!"

He scratched his wrist under the cuff of the chain attached to the boat. Two months he'd been like this. It was all a misunderstanding.

*

Samuel was washing the deck on the ship while Pierce, a tall man and expert fisher, was losing at a card game. Hushed accusations became louder, and soon Pierce and a man named

Crocket were at each other's throats. A melee broke out, and Samuel grabbed the bucket he was using.

He swung the bucket wildly, trying to break up the fisticuffs. On one downward swing, he struck Pierce on the head. It was an accident. Pierce not only lost his money, but also his life as he fell to the deck. Pierce was dead, and Samuel was in irons.

Samuel reflected on this as he listened to the rain. He reached out for the mug. After a long drink, he replaced the mug and thought of his first days on the island.

The captain was a right hard bastard. He was also greedy as hell. The last thing he wanted was to go back to Scotland for a trial and waste the summer with no fishing. Samuel didn't know who came up with the idea of abandoning him on this island, but it struck the captain as sound.

"If I find out who the bastard was, I will spend a whole summer waiting just to kill him."

When they arrived at the island, the sailors pulled the large rowboat beyond the beach, onto the hard sand. Happy that Samuel wasn't strong enough to move the boat back down to the water, they chained him to the rowboat and put a meager amount of food and water just out of reach. The sailors laughed as Samuel tried to pull the heavy rowboat towards the food. Every time he got close, the sailors would grab the food and water and place it further away. The game went on for hours until a gunshot from the ship signaled the sailors to return. They moved the food once more and returned to the ship, laughing all the way back.

"We will see you in a couple of months," they yelled. Samuel didn't bother watching them go. He pulled the rowboat towards the food one last time. He was so exhausted he could hardly eat. He flipped the boat over and brought the food inside. It rained hard, and a lot of water ran under the boat. Samuel was in misery.

*

The rain was heavier now, and Samuel grabbed the mug. He drank all of it in one gulp and replaced the mug. He may have been starving, but at least the water was keeping him alive. The rain was also a relief from the flies, although he knew they would be back in droves in the morning.

He wondered if Pierce was out there in the rain. He first saw the man a month after he was imprisoned. The tall man just stared at him. It was also the first time he saw the silver wolf. No doubt hanging around for an easy meal.

Samuel gazed out from under the boat and saw the dead man. He was standing by the big rocks just on shore. The spectre just stared at him. Samuel rolled onto his back. He kept telling himself it was the starvation that caused him to see Pierce. He grabbed the mug once more and swallowed. He lay back and let sleep overwhelm him.

*

Samuel was awakened by voices. He shook his head. Suddenly the boat flipped over, and Samuel was looking at three faces. They were laughing.

"The bastard's still alive."

Samuel was grabbed and lifted to his feet. The three sailors punched him in the gut. Samuel dropped to his knees.

"Get his boots," one of the sailors yelled. Samuel was kicked over onto his back as two of his attackers wrenched the boots off. Samuel was too weak to fight them.

"Captain says we have to leave you some food," the lead sailor said, as he walked a good hundred yards away. He put the meager supplies down on a rock and returned.

"Captain says if you're still alive in another month, you're coming back to Scotland and you're going on trial."

"Murderer," another sailor said.

A gunshot from the ship got the sailors' attention. They each kicked Samuel one last time and returned to their rowboat. They were back on board the ship before Samuel had recovered enough to take in his predicament.

"Christ almighty."

Samuel stared at the supplies. Taking a deep breath, he pushed himself up and steadied himself against the rowboat. He pulled at the cuff on his wrist. Two months of starving, with the occasional raw rat or seabird to help stave it off, was not enough for him to slip his wrist out.

He resigned himself to his fate and stumbled to the bow of the boat. He grabbed the boat, took a deep breath, and pulled. The boat barely moved and inch. After a second attempt, Samuel collapsed. He turned to see Pierce standing on the other side of the food.

Pierce was dressed as he was on the day he died: shirt and pants and decent boots. His shaggy beard was as clean as his bald head. The dead man was staring at him, mocking him, almost laughing at his situation.

"Why don't you go away? Haven't I been punished enough?"

Pierce was unmoved. Samuel got up and pulled again. It moved half a foot.

"See? See? I still got some strength left."

Emboldened, Samuel pulled again at the boat. The food was coming closer. His feet started to blister against the rocks as he tugged. The flies bit at his ravaged skin as he pulled harder. When he felt he was close enough, Samuel let go of the boat and walked the length of his chain. He was still two feet away.

He went back to the boat, intending to continue, but stopped short. Gazing down, Samuel found the boat had brought up against a large rock in the sand. Samuel moaned and cursed. Losing his temper, the man turned towards his silent visitor and yelled, "Help me you bastard!"

Pierce stood perfectly still. Samuel looked down at the stone. He knew he wouldn't be able to move it, so he would have to go around it. With an effort, he dragged the boat towards the side of the stone. It was hard going, as the rowboat would rock back and forth before moving. Several minutes of effort finally succeeded in moving the boat to the side of the stone.

Samuel cried out in triumph. He cursed Pierce, and started to haul the boat again. The hard sand helped slide it, and soon he was close enough. He needed to rest, and sat down next to the boat, closing his eyes. After several minutes, Samuel opened them. To his horror, he spied the wolf trotting towards him up the beach. Pierce smiled.

Samuel got to his feet and stumbled towards the food. The chain brought up just inches away. Samuel screamed in frustration, his hoarse voice sounding through the wilderness. With both hands, he grabbed the chain and pulled. He only needed a couple of inches. His back roared in pain and his legs started to cramp.

The boat jerked forward. Samuel turned to reach for the food but was met with the jaws of the wolf, who bit down on his hand. Samuel screamed and pulled his hand away. The wolf grabbed the small sack of food, and Samuel yelled at the animal as it trotted away.

"The hell with you!"

He reached for the small flask of water. As he grabbed it, his hand was shaking so hard from the wolf's bite that he dropped it out of reach and all the water spilled. Samuel watched it sink into the sand and started to laugh. He pointed at the water and turned to Pierce. The ghost was smiling.

Hours later, it rained, and Samuel huddled in the rowboat, too weak to flip it over. Pierce stood next to him. As he sat there drenched, Samuel said to his spectral visitor, "I didn't mean to kill you."

Pierce stared at him. He was now covered in blood from a vicious head wound.

"I was just trying to break up the fight. I'm sorry I hit you."

Pierce continued to stare at him.

"Is this punishment enough for you?" Pierce answered by pointing at the cuff on Samuel's wrist. Samuel looked at the cuff and pulled at it. His skin was soaked, and the cuff started to cut through his skin. Samuel moved the cuff back and forth, slicing more skin but getting a little further with it. Pierce watched.

The bitten hand throbbed as Samuel pulled. The chain cut more skin, and finally, with one final effort, it slid through the cuff. Samuel looked at his free hand. He started to laugh. With his remaining strength, he heaved himself out of the boat and onto the sand. He leapt up and yelled at Pierce, "Pierce! I'm free. The hell with you and the captain and his bastard sailors."

He turned and ran up the beach, forgetting the ghost. As he ran, Samuel screamed at the sky and the sea. Eventually he stopped, and gazed at the sea and the pouring rain. He heard the padding of feet. He turned to see several wolves staring at him.

"The silver's pack."

He noticed they were different colours. White, black, and a mixture of both. He started running, and they trotted along with him, knowing the easy meal that was to come. Samuel laughed out loud as he continued to run.

*

A month later, when the captain and his ship returned to the island, his sailors found the empty rowboat and the bloody chain. They found blood further up the beach, but no other sign of Samuel.

After reporting this to the captain, he and the first mate chose one of the other men, a simple man from St. Mirren's, to be tried for the murder of Pierce in place of Samuel. The crew made no effort to resist the decision.

As the ship pulled away, Pierce stood on the beach alongside the silver wolf. They both showed signs of contentment.

Unnatural Transport

Somewhere in Quebec, 1941

Dusk was settling in when the train pulled away from the small, out-of-the-way train depot. It had only taken forty-five minutes to add the extra baggage car, but to the soldiers of the Lincoln and Welland Regiment, it added to the hours-long journey.

Sgt. Chamberlin stepped into the car his platoon was occupying and shook his head. The orders he'd just received from the Major made no sense. The soldiers noticed the strange look on their leader's face. Chamberlin stood at the front of the car and addressed his men:

"Boys, that extra baggage car we just picked up apparently contains some special or important items, and the Chief Engineer of this lovely train has instructed our Major to post a guard at the end of our car."

The soldiers looked around at each other with puzzled faces.

"What good is that going to do, Sarge?" a small private in the back named Parsons asked.

"Good question, but orders are orders," Chamberlin answered. "Any volunteers?"

"How about old Collins back there, Sarge? His ears are so big they would block the door with him sitting down,"

Corporal Skinner piped up. The cocky young man had a huge grin on his face.

"That's funny, Skinner," Collins said, sitting up and pulling a pipe out of his mouth. "You should be a stand-up comedian."

"Well, I don't mean to brag, but when I'm on stage and there are a lot of women in the audience, I'm not the only thing that stands up, if you know what I mean," Skinner bragged.

"I bet that gets the audience laughing," Parsons said from the back, and the car erupted in laughter.

Chamberlin bit his lip to keep from laughing as well, as Skinner flipped an obscene gesture back at his pals. When the laughter petered out, Chamberlin said to Skinner, "Well, since you know so much about stand-up, you can go 'stand up' at the back door."

Skinner hung his head for a moment, grabbed his rifle and walked to the back of the car. Chamberlin smiled to himself as he turned and made his way to the front. He sat down, taking his helmet off and laying it on the empty seat next to him. While the rest of the platoon were crammed next to each other, being a Sergeant, he had a little extra room.

"Rank does have its privileges," he said, as he leaned his head back.

An hour later, the door at the front of the car opened, and the platoon commander, Lt. Rochester, entered and sat next to Chamberlin. Night had fallen outside, and the interior lights hadn't been turned on yet, so most of the men were either sleeping or chatting quietly. The Lt. leaned over to Chamberlin and whispered, "What do you know about the extra car we picked up?"

Chamberlin shook his head.

"Well, there are rumours floating around in the front about something sinister in that car. Did you notice anything unusual?"

Chamberlin rubbed his eyes and took a deep breath. He liked Rochester, but found him a little jumpy.

"The only strange thing I noticed was a tall man dressed in black, wearing a long cloak and top hat, standing next to the car. He seemed to be supervising the hook-up."

Rochester nodded and lost himself in thought. Chamberlin gazed at his Lt. He was a thin man with coal black hair and a pencil mustache. To Chamberlin, Rochester looked as if he was always thinking. He rarely talked to the troops and kept mostly to himself. Chamberlin's dad once told him that when a man starts thinking too much, the outside world falls away.

Chamberlin waited until the Lt. finished his inner analyzing. Finally, Rochester spoke:

"Apparently, we are dropping the car in New Brunswick. Destination unknown. The gentleman you mentioned is in the lead car, conversing with the Engineer. The stranger also wants to sit back here with the platoon to watch over the car. Who do you have on the door?"

"Skinner. He's a good man, despite his poor sense of humour. I was going to have him relieved in a bit."

"No, keep him there until the stranger arrives. Skinner has a lot of experience; the rest of the men in the platoon are quite young," Rochester advised.

"What does the Major think?" Chamberlin asked.

"Major Hamilton is dismissive of all concerns. He is currently in the dining car enjoying his Port and chicken legs. Keep me informed." Rochester got up. "The stranger should be back here within the hour."

Chamberlin gave a quick salute as Rochester vanished through the front door. Chamberlin stood up and gazed over his troops. They *were* a good lot, but Rochester was right. They were young. Too young to be heading to the hell which was Europe. He was about to sit down again when the door to the car opened.

Chamberlin turned to see the tall man who accompanied the extra car. His imposing height was exaggerated by his tall black hat. He wore a long cloak that covered his feet, and his long face was covered with a scraggly beard. The dark eyes in the centre of his face scowled over his long nose. The man was the opposite of Chamberlin, whose stout five-foot-ten frame and round but hard face gave him the air of authority. The tall man had the the air of someone to be feared.

"Good day, Sir," Chamberlin addressed the tall man. "Are you the owner of the extra car?"

The tall man nodded. Chamberlin waited for an answer. When none came, he continued, "May I have your name, Sir? It's only so I know what to call you in case of an emergency."

The tall man stared off into space. The pause hung in the air like a heavy fog. Chamberlin glanced at his troops. The alert soldiers woke their buddies as they stared at the stranger. Skinner had his rifle at the ready.

"You may call me…Mr. Fox." The answer resonated throughout the car.

"Well, Mr. Fox, according to my superiors, you are going to be riding with us. Is there anywhere specific you would like to sit?"

"The back," Fox answered.

Chamberlin turned and waved to the two privates sitting in the rear seats. As they moved, Fox walked towards the end of the car. The platoon stared at the tall man. It seemed to Chamberlin that Fox glided down the car instead of walking. The two privates at the back pressed themselves to the side of the seats as Fox passed them.

Skinner never took his eyes off Fox, who turned and sat down in the last seat. His rifle was at the ready as Fox reached inside his cloak and pulled out a pair of small, rounded sunglasses.

Chamberlin nodded at Parsons. The private got the message, retrieved his rifle, and lay it across his lap. The two privates found new seats, and Chamberlin slowly sat back in his. As the interior lights came on, Chamberlin pulled his shaving mirror out of his kit and hung it in a strategic position on the wall in front of him. He adjusted it so he could see Fox.

Corporal Skinner kept throwing side glances at Fox as he stood by the door. The man gave him the creeps. Skinner was reminded of those old folk tales his mother would tell him of a hairy beast that walked through the woods in Northern British Columbia, and stories of sea monsters on the Atlantic coast that were told to him by his uncle from Newfoundland. To Skinner, Mr. Fox gave off a 'Jack the Ripper' vibe, and the young corporal felt a chill go up his back.

The full moon was hanging in the dark sky when Skinner heard the first noises from the extra car. At first, he thought the loud scratching and moaning was coming from the train itself as it moved along the rails. He also thought he heard cries of pain and grunting. Skinner shot a sideways glance at Fox, who was staring forward.

Skinner looked towards the front, and saw Chamberlin standing up to stretch. Skinner motioned to him, and Chamberlin was soon walking towards him.

"What's up?" Chamberlin asked.

"Listen," Skinner answered, and nodded his head towards the door.

Chamberlin leaned in but heard nothing. When he pulled back, he saw the look of concern on Skinner's face. When Chamberlin gave his Corporal a questioning look, Skinner leaned towards him and described the noises. Chamberlin gave a slight glance at Fox.

"OK. It could be nothing, but keep at the ready. If you hear anything else, yell."

Skinner acknowledged Chamberlin, and the Sergeant walked back to his seat. When he sat down, Chamberlin thought about Skinner. He had nerves of steel and was a good man, not easily spooked. However, this Fox character and his car had everyone on edge. He turned to face the window, and watched the full moonlight dance off the nearby lake.

An hour later, Skinner heard the sounds again. He stepped forward from the door and turned. He held his rifle at the ready position. Parsons slowly got out of his seat and joined Skinner.

"Go get the Sarge," Skinner said. Parsons headed towards the front of the car. Most of the men were sleeping at this point, but Chamberlin was reading a book. He looked up when Parsons arrived. Parsons motioned to Skinner, and Chamberlin was out of his chair. Moments later, Skinner was updating the two of them.

"Scratching. Lots of it."

Chamberlin walked to the door and listened. There was loud scratching and for a second, he heard moaning. He whispered to Skinner and Parsons, "Wake everyone up and be at the ready."

When the two soldiers left to carry out their orders, Chamberlin turned to Mr. Fox.

"Alright, Sir, it's one thing to be secretive about your cargo when it isn't a threat; it's another when it is. What the hell is that car carrying?"

Mr. Fox casually rotated his head, stretching his neck, then stood up.

"There's no need to wake everyone. They are contained back there."

"What's contained?" Chamberlin asked.

"My passengers," Fox answered.

"Not good enough. What's back there?" Chamberlin asked with an authoritarian tone.

"*Loup garou.*"

Chamberlin shot Fox a questionable look. Before he could ask, a voice came from behind him.

"Werewolves."

Chamberlin turned to see another young private, Elgin Benoit.

"It's French for werewolves."

Chamberlin nodded to Benoit and turned back to Fox. He didn't believe in such things, but current events had him questioning that belief. Fox addressed the Sergeant, a calm look on his face. "They are contained. They may make some noise, but they are not going anywhere."

"Why are they there to begin with?" Skinner asked.

Fox looked around the car at the soldiers staring at him. Not wanting any trouble, he answered, "Fine." After pausing to take a deep breath, Fox continued. "The world has many mysteries. Some of you believe in them, some of you don't, but believe me when I say that such creatures exist and, from time to time, need transportation. That's where I come in."

Chamberlin stared at Fox. "Creatures?"

"Yes," Fox said. "Two, what did you call them? Ah yes, werewolves."

"Well, if it's true about these loop-whatever-the-fuck, why are they travelling with the full moon?" Parsons asked, as he and Skinner returned.

"Good opportunity for travelling, since you are going the same way," Fox answered. "As for the full moon, that's nonsense. Werewolves can change anytime they like. The full moon tonight is a coincidence. Something must have set them off."

"What could set them off?" Skinner asked.

"Anything. Right now, it could be hunger. I don't know when was the last time they ate."

"What do you mean, you don't know? I thought you said you looked after their travel arrangements?" Skinner pressed.

"I only showed up with the carriage. What happened before that is none of my concern."

"Well, it looks like it *could* become your concern," Skinner added.

"What happens if they get out?" Chamberlin asked.

"They're not going to get out," Fox answered.

"Humour me," Chamberlin countered.

"If they get out, well, there are a lot of people on this train they could eat," Fox answered coldly.

"How do we kill them?" Parsons asked.

"Silver bullet?" Skinner chimed in.

Fox scoffed. "Silver bullet? That's another myth. They die just like anyone else. Are your men armed?"

Chamberlin blew out a breath and shook his head.

"No. We are to be supplied in Halifax before we get on the boat."

"Bayonets?" Skinner asked.

Fox nodded. Chamberlin gave the order to have them at the ready.

"Are they contained?" Chamberlin asked Fox.

"Contained," Fox said.

Satisfied with what he heard, Chamberlin left to go back to his seat. He told Benoit to relive Skinner on the door, informed the rest of the platoon to got back to sleep, and fished out his book. Fox sat down and Benoit took Skinner's place at the door.

Chamberlin had only read two lines on the page before Skinner addressed him.

"I don't like this one bit, Sarge."

"I don't like it either, but that's the cards we've been dealt," he paused. "You and Parsons are senior, so let the men sleep, and the two of you keep an eye on things. Hopefully we have a quiet night."

Skinner nodded and left. Agitated, Chamberlin put away his book, leaned back, and closed his eyes. Sleep didn't come. Frustrated, he got up and glanced back at his men. The heaviness of taking these young men to war was starting to weigh on him. While most of the men were sleeping, Chamberlin noticed Private Rogers was staring out the window.

Chamberlin thought about the man for a minute. Rogers, from Port Colborne on the shores of Lake Erie, was an athletic man and a real storyteller. He was fun to be around, but also a very hard worker. He was slated to be promoted when they got to Halifax.

However, Chamberlin had noticed a real change in Rogers. Just before they boarded the train, Rogers became very stoic. He hardly spoke to anyone, and he had lost his charm. Parsons had mentioned it as they passed Kingston, but explained it away by saying it was nerves, which most of the men had. Now, with all the crap with the extra car, Chamberlin glanced at Rogers' reflection in the window. His eyes just stared off into the distance. It was as if the young man wasn't in his body.

*

Benoit kept one eye on the door and the other on Fox. The scratching had started again, but with more urgency. Fox just kept staring straight ahead, and didn't acknowledge the noise. Benoit gripped his rifle and was starting to sweat. After a few moments, the scratching stopped, and he relaxed. He let out a long breath and closed his eyes.

"Thank Christ," he said out loud.

A thunderous bang sounded as the rear door flew off its hinges and crashed into the platoon car. Benoit was thrown off his feet, and everyone in the car was now awake. Chamberlin raced to the end of the car in time to help Skinner and Parsons raise Benoit to his feet. He turned to Fox.

"I think your idea of containment is a little flawed!"

Fox stood up and glanced at the back door. In the gloom, the group saw two pairs of eyes looking back at them. Chamberlin stepped in front of his soldiers and held his rifle at the ready. The two pairs of eyes stepped out of the rear car; they were attached to two large bipedal wolves who snarled at them.

"What the hell, Fox?!" Chamberlin exclaimed.

Fox stood silent. He stared at the wolves, who ignored the men and leapt onto the exterior side of the train. Skinner ran to the middle of the car and looked up. Chamberlin and the platoon did the same. Stomping feet could be heard on the roof.

"Guard the front door!" Chamberlin yelled.

Skinner grabbed a private and they rushed to the front. As they arrived, Lt. Rochester stepped through the door. He barely had time to open his mouth when he was grabbed from behind and disappeared back through the door.

"Holy Jesus!" Skinner yelled.

"Shut the door!" Chamberlin yelled.

Skinner slammed the door shut. "What about the Lt.?!" he shouted back.

Chamberlin was about to answer when he saw Rochester fly off the train and land heavily on the ground.

"Just keep the door shut!" he shouted back.

Skinner and the private, a man named Jones, slammed the door and engaged the lock. The sound of smashing glass got their attention as the wolves on either side of the train were smashing the windows to get back in.

"Defend the car!" Chamberlin yelled, and the platoon slashed at the hairy arms of a werewolf trying to get inside. Chamberlin turned to Fox. "What the hell?"

Fox glanced around at the fighting. "I know what they're after."

Chamberlin turned to where Fox was pointing. It was Rogers, just standing in the middle of the car. He dropped his rifle and started to tremble. The fighting slowed as the platoon turned to look at Rogers. Soon his whole body was shaking, and his skin broke apart. A terrifying scream emitted from Rogers as the skin slid off his body, revealing a grotesque creature inhabiting the skeleton.

The half-dressed monster lashed out and drove its razor-sharp bony fingers into the closest private. Blood shot out of the man's neck and covered the windows as he fell to the floor. Bayonets slashed at the creature to little effect. Chamberlin leapt onto a seat and drove his bayonet into the creature's head. Again, it had no effect. He turned and saw the wolves smashing at the windows.

"Skinner, open the door!"

Skinner nodded, ran to the door and disengaged the locks. As soon as the door opened, the wolves rushed in, knocking Skinner aside. The wolves joined in on the attack as Chamberlin yelled out once more, "Skinner, unhook the car!"

Skinner understood the command and ran out to the coupling. He unhooked the cables, extinguishing the lights in the car. Using the butt of his rifle, Skinner smashed the coupling until it released. He glanced up to see the faces of the other men look at him as the train pulled away. Skinner took a couple of breaths and re-entered the car.

Chaos reigned as the fight continued. Another private was wounded, and the soldiers slashed at the creature in the dark. The wolves knocked some of the soldiers aside as they bit into the creature. An unearthly scream sounded in the car as creature fell over, dead on the floor. As the wolves stood over it, the creature's body dissolved into a mist, floating out the window as the two cars slowed to a stop.

Silence filled the car as the men caught their breath, stared at the empty uniform of Rogers. Chamberlin stepped forward.

"Everyone out of the car. Skinner, you and Parsons set up a sentry." Skinner acknowledged the command and led everyone off. The wolves sniffed at the uniform. Satisfied, the two wolves shuffled out of the train and ran off into the wilderness. Chamberlin turned to Fox.

"What the hell was that?"

"I don't know. Whatever it was, it didn't come from our world. The wolves must have sensed its coming and quickly arranged this transport." After a pause he said, "I am sorry about your men."

Chamberlin's thoughts went to the dead private, and the wounded man now being treated outside. He turned to see Fox head for the door.

"Where are you going? I need you to help explain this," Chamberlin said.

"Sorry, I only look after the transportation. Now that there is no one to transport, my job is done, and I have other commitments that have just come to my attention."

Before Chamberlin could say anything, Fox stepped through the door and disappeared. Chamberlin stepped outside and glanced up the track. He could see the train backing up to get them. Chamberlin sighed and waved to Parsons and Skinner. When they arrived, he said, "So, how do we explain this?"

The two corporals shrugged, and Chamberlin closed his eyes.

"How's Private Olsen?"

"Fine, but he will need some more medical attention," Parsons answered.

"The private who was killed?"

"Private Beecham," Skinner replied. "We took a head count. Everyone else has been accounted for."

Chamberlin nodded and dismissed the men. How was he going to explain two dead men and one wounded? They also had to go back and get the Lt. As the train neared, he glanced off into the hills. Under the light of the full moon, he spotted two silhouettes. Despite the carnage, the wolves had saved their lives. He gave them a small wave, and they vanished into the woods.

He also thought of Fox. In the back of his mind, Chamberlin got the feeling it wouldn't be the last time he lay eyes on him. As the train arrived, Chamberlin remembered what his father told him: "The truth, my son, is better than any lie. No matter what the truth is."

As Major Hamilton strutted up to Chamberlin he thought, *Well, Dad, the truth in this case is a real doozy.*

The Not-So-OK Corral

Sheriff Watkins stepped out of his office and walked to the train station just outside the town, the telegraph message still in his hand. At fifty-five, Watkins was feeling his age, and the urgency of the town's situation weighed heavily on his shoulders.

As the sun settled in the west behind the city, Watkins spied the train rumbling its way towards the station. Watkins wiped the sweat from his eyes and replaced his glasses. As the train pulled in, Watkins glanced down at the message.

'Acknowledged. A Mr. MacDaniel and partner will arrive 10 Aug in the evening.'

"Right on time."

Steam flooded the station as the train groaned to a halt. A couple of minutes later, several passengers disembarked. Watkins nodded to several of them. As the station cleared, the last two passengers stepped onto the platform. The sheriff had never seen anything like it.

Despite the heat of the evening, the visitors wore leather suits with matching long coats. They both wore wide-brimmed hats and leather boots, with six-shooters on their belts and dark glasses hiding their eyes. They each carried a black sack. It was at that moment that Watkins noticed the second rider was a woman. The man stood in front of the sheriff and extended his right hand.

"Sheriff Watkins, my name is Hugo MacDaniel. My partner, Francine Bellecourt."

Watkins shook Hugo's hand and nodded to Francine. He led the two visitors out of the station and into the town. Hugo noticed the large sign:

'Welcome to Dead Bull, Texas.'

Watkins saw the look on Hugo's face as he spotted the sign.

"Fellow who founded this place was prospecting when his donkey, who was carrying his equipment, just up and died."

"Why didn't he call it 'Dead Donkey'?" Francine asked.

"This is Texas—it wasn't manly enough," Hugo answered.

Watkins stayed silent as he led them to his office. Hugo glanced up the street at some townsfolk who'd spotted him and Francine. He noticed that they'd started to whisper to themselves. Francine touched his arm, turning him away from the crowd, and the two of them followed the sheriff into the building.

The Sheriff's office contained two desks, a firearms lockup, a wood stove, and down a small hallway, two jail cells. Hugo took note of several pictures of wanted men on the wall surrounding a picture of President James Garfield. Francine walked over to the far side of the room, dropped her sack on the floor, and threw herself into one of the three chairs available. Hugo continued to stand.

Watkins offered whiskey, but it was declined. He poured himself a large glass and sat at his desk. After taking a deep drink, he put the glass on his desk and addressed his visitors.

"First, thank you very much for coming on such short notice. We have a problem that is a bit above us, and we need people with your unique talents."

Francine nodded while Hugo stood motionless. Watkins continued:

"Three weeks ago, a stagecoach came into town. It's a rare occurrence due to the frequency of the train."

Hugo listened intently to Watkins. The stagecoach was pulled by four black horses, and its windows were covered. The driver, a tall, expensively dressed man, stepped down and reported to the sheriff's office. The driver required accommodations, but the passengers were to stay inside the coach.

"When we inquired about the passengers, the driver explained that they were suffering from a rare contagious disease. We eventually put the coach in an old barn at the far end of the town. The horses were squared away, and the driver took a room in our hotel at the crossroads of the town.

"The driver assured us that the passengers had food and water, but that it would need to be replenished every couple of days."

Watkins paused to finish his whiskey and refill the glass.

"Everything was fine at first. The driver, whose name is Donavan, brought food and drink to the coach every couple of days. He had plenty of money, and didn't cause any disturbance. On the fourth night, a gentleman named Lake made a complaint to me about strange noises coming from the barn in the middle of the night."

"What was he doing out at the barn in the middle of the night?" Francine asked.

"He was drunk. At first, we ignored him, but soon the noises became louder, and residents of nearby houses brought it forward to me. I asked Donavan, who explained that the passengers suffered greatly from their ailment and couldn't sleep. Hence the cries at night."

Hugo stared at Watkins as he continued. "We took his word for it. I mean, outside of the cries at night, there was no trouble."

"I take it that changed two weeks ago," Francine said.

Watkins nodded, finished his whiskey, and stood up.

"I guess the best way to explain this is to see Doc Elliot."

*

Dr. Elliot's office was on the north corner of the crossroads at the centre of town. Doc 'Dutch' Elliot was a squat, round man who, in a small town, specialized in every complaint. Francine noted eyeglasses, powders and liquids, bandages, and a small operating table at the back. She also noted several surgical instruments with specks of blood on them. Watkins had briefed Elliot, who led them to a back room.

"I've never seen anything like this before," Elliot said, opening the door. "I hid the bodies back here until I could get some clarification from Houston."

Watkins covered his nose as he walked into the room. The air was rancid, but Elliot noticed that the smell didn't bother Hugo or Francine. He bent down and pulled the sheets off the bodies. Watkins winced at the sight.

Hugo walked around the bodies, studying them. Francine did the same on the opposite side of the room.

"Who was the first victim?" Hugo asked.

"Jack Thompson," Watkins answered. "Happened the night after the mass complaints. He lived near the barn with his wife. He must have gotten fed up with the sounds. We found him just outside the barn door."

"Second victim?" Hugo asked.

"Susan Wells," Elliot answered. "Local, ah, *lady of the evening*." Francine smiled to herself as Elliot blushed.

"We think she was in the wrong place at the wrong time," Watkins said.

"Or maybe she was looking to make some money," Francine added.

Hugo continued to stare at the victims. Even with the decomposition, he was able to determine their fates. After a few minutes of silence, he spoke.

"Any other unusual disturbances?"

Watkins hesitated as he looked at Elliot.

"Well, over the last couple of weeks, I and others have noticed certain people staying inside all day."

"I mean, it's one thing if they're sick and stay home for a couple of days, but it's been two weeks and we haven't seen our local tailor, one of the school governesses, and several of the local workmen," Elliot added.

Francine and Hugo exchanged glances. With a nod to her, he said, "I think it's time we spoke to this Donavan."

*

The bland sign above the door stated the obvious: 'Hotel and Saloon'. Watkins led his visitors inside. Despite the deaths in the town, the place was lively. Francine walked over to the bar and removed her hat. Her red, curly hair fell over her shoulders. This action caught the attention of several drunken louts who undressed her with their eyes.

Watkins pointed Donavan out to Hugo. The man was sitting at the back of the room, sipping a beer. Hugo slowly walked towards him, aware that some of the patrons were staring at him. When he reached the table, Hugo asked, "Join you for a drink? My treat."

Donavan nodded, and Hugo motioned to Watkins. Hugo sat down opposite the driver and stared at him. Donavan was a lackey and, although his clothes were nice, Hugo could tell that Donavan wasn't used to wearing them. The shaving nicks on his face betrayed the fact that he usually wore a beard.

When Watkins brought the drinks, Hugo accepted his whiskey and swallowed it in one go. He put the glass down on the table and asked in a low voice, "Who are your passengers? Did they kill those two people?"

Donavan stared down at his near empty glass and shrugged.

"Where are they going?"

Donavan remained silent. Hugo sat back in his chair.

"I've seen the bodies. I know how they died."

"You don't know anything," Donavan said.

Hugo leaned forward on the table. "I know they only attack at night, and rip out their victims' throats."

Donavan finished his beer and grabbed the second glass. Hugo pressed on.

"A lack of blood in the bodies. Come on, my friend. Who's paying you to transport these monsters?"

Watkins leaned forward and stared at Donavan. The man was sweating. Hugo persisted.

"Are they from New Orleans?"

Donavan lowered his head.

"Did Romero pay you?" Hugo pressed.

Donavan snapped his head up. Hugo smiled.

"Who's Romero?" Watkins asked.

"Someone you never want to encounter," Hugo answered. To Donavan, he continued, "He paid you to get those two out of Louisiana, didn't he? Lay low for a while."

"He'd kill me if anything went wrong," Donavan said, his voice shaking. He looked up at Hugo, his reflection in the bald man's glasses. "He gave me enough money for three months."

"Just enough time for things to be smoothed over. What happened? Didn't feed them enough?"

Donavan opened his mouth and shut it again. After a minute he said, "I followed every instruction. Did everything I was asked. I don't know what happened."

Hugo nodded and turned to Watkins.

"Let's bring him back to the office. Not so many ears there."

Watkins stood up and took Donavan gently by the arm. Hugo followed, gesturing to Francine, who was being harassed by one of the locals. When the man leaned in for a kiss, Francine's hand flew to the side of his head, slamming it down on the bar. She gazed around the room as the man slid to the floor.

Hugo smiled as Francine paid for her drink, picked up her hat, and followed the three men out of the saloon.

*

"You have to remember there is no set way to deal with these creatures," Hugo said to Donavan, once they were back in the sheriff's office. "It doesn't matter how well you feed them; their bloodlust will always win out."

Donavan downed his whiskey in one gulp and waved the glass so Watkins could refill it. Francine sat in the corner, quietly observing the events. Hugo waited until the sheriff refilled the glass before continuing.

"Newly transformed?" he asked.

Donavan nodded and gulped his whiskey.

"How long?" Hugo asked.

"Maybe a couple of months," Donavan answered.

Hugo frowned and glanced at Francine. She gave him a slight nod in agreement. Hugo turned again to Donavan.

"Who turned them?"

Donavan stared at his glass, the warped reflection showing his future. He closed his eyes and spoke. "Someone new. She came down from the north."

"Name," Hugo demanded.

"Serena. No last name, just Serena."

Francine jumped up. She grabbed Donavan by the hair and pulled his head back.

"Do you know how many people these creatures have killed?"

"No!" Donavan croaked out.

"Twenty. The people of Baton Rouge are calling for all our heads. Vampires and hunters. Romero and his clan have royally fucked all of us!"

Francine threw his head forward and walked out of the room. Hugo stared down at the man. He knew Donavan's status amongst the vampires. Though he didn't kill anyone, he was still involved.

"Francine is right. Everyone in Louisianna is walking on eggshells. Anyone suspected of not being normal is being killed. This 'Serena' may have endangered us all."

Donavan began to weep.

"Who does Romero have over you?" Hugo asked.

"My sister, Caroline," Donavon said, pulling a chain out of his pocket. He opened the locket, which contained the picture of a young blond-haired woman.

Hugo turned to Watkins.

"Sheriff, round up about ten of your best men. We have a nasty job ahead of us."

*

It was dark when the group was organized. Watkins informed Hugo that the men were either ranchers or tradesmen, hard men who could handle themselves. Francine smiled at Hugo, who was equally impressed.

Hugo explained the matter, and there were some questions.

"Why attack now instead of the morning? Three reasons. One, according to Donavan, they fed last night so their hunger may be satiated. Two, most people will be inside—fewer witnesses, less potential collateral damage. Three, if anyone else in town has been changed, they will come out, revealing themselves. We don't want to conduct a search during the day and kill someone who was innocently sick."

"Load up your weapons, men," Watkins said, coming out of the office and carrying ammunition. He distributed the ammo and looked at Hugo.

He and Francine had shed their long coats. They each wore two crossed swords on their backs, belts with six-shooters, and two handheld crossbows. Watkins also noticed a variety of knives holstered around their bodies. He looked down at his two six-shooters and felt very naked.

"Remember one thing—if you encounter any of your friends who have been turned, as hard as it's going to be, they are *already dead*. You will be doing them a favour by destroying them."

"Bullets will kill them?" one of the men asked.

"No," Hugo answered. "However, a bullet will stun them and slow them down."

"The woman? Are we going to need to protect her?" asked a huge man at the back.

Francine walked up to the big man and gave him a seductive look. When the man smiled at her, Francine reached out, grabbed him by the balls, and squeezed. The man gasped and she grabbed him by the shirt, pulling his face down to hers.

"Maybe you're the one who needs protecting, hey sweetie?"

The group laughed, and even Hugo smiled to himself. Francine released the man and turned away as he fell to his knees. Francine looked at the group and cocked her eyebrows. The message was loud and clear. Hugo turned to Watkins.

"Alright, let's go. Donavan, you stay here," he said. Donavan acknowledged the order, retreating into the Sheriff's office, while the rest headed into town.

*

Francine glanced up at the full moon and thought it was the perfect cliché for the moment. She walked two steps behind the group. Not for her protection, but for theirs. The surrounding buildings stood silent, and all of her senses were heightened.

She turned at the sound of footsteps on a rooftop to her left, and crouched, grabbing her crossbows. Her keen eyesight spotted the culprit, a black cat. Francine blew out a breath and smiled. She straightened, and was about to put her crossbows away when she heard a hiss from behind her. She dropped back into a crouch and fired a bolt between the eyes of a female vampire who was stalking up behind them.

The vampire stood stunned for a moment before her head exploded. The men turned to see the vampire fall. Francine stood up, walked over to the corpse, and picked up the arrow. To the men she said, "Arrows dipped in holy water. Nasty stuff."

Behind the group, a skinny man with a tall hat led another man pulling a wagon. Francine spoke to the man, "Ah, I was wondering if the Undertaker would be out." Pointing to the corpse, she added, "Burn that, will you?"

The Undertaker and his assistant picked up the body and laid it in the wagon. Francine turned to the men, who were looking at her, their mouths open. With a nod of her head, she urged them on to the barn.

Watkins was sweating. In all his years of living in the west and being sheriff, the worst he'd ever encountered was cattle rustlers and the odd drunk in town. This was above him and he was frightened. Hugo walked up to him.

"I can feel your fear. Don't worry, I value someone who is fearful rather than overconfident. Keeps your senses sharp."

Watkins blew out a breath, and Hugo placed a hand on his shoulder. The group carried on with no other incident. As they approached the barn, they heard a loud disturbance coming from the corral just off the back end. The horses were kicking and whinnying. The group ran to the corral to see a horrifying sight.

"My good Christ!" one of men whispered.

Several people, all recently changed, were attacking the horses. The men aimed and fired at the scene. The explosion of gunfire sounded through the town, and Hugo noticed the lighting of lamps in several windows. Shrieks of pain echoed out into the wilderness as the last of the horses and creatures fell.

The silence was deafening. Hugo and Francine stepped into the corral and finished the task. The Undertaker stood silently as the two hunters exited the corral. As Hugo led Francine back to the group, another group of men strode forward with a very dazed Donavan between them. He looked beaten up, no doubt from being dragged from the Sheriff's office.

This new group's leader, a rancher named Sullivan, shouted at the hunters, "Here, you unholy henchmen. If you're going in that barn to kill those monsters, take this wretched thing with you. He brought this upon our town!"

The sheriff's group shouted in agreement.

"He's responsible for the death of several good men and women, as well as a few strong horses!"

The entire group started to clamour, and soon, other people from town began to show up. Hugo looked at the beaten-up Donavan and sighed. He had no choice. He raised his hands to the crowd and said in a soothing but authoritative voice, "We will take him with us."

The crowd fell into an uneasy silence, unsure how to react. Hugo walked over and grabbed Donavan. He led him towards the barn and joined Francine at the door. As they were about to enter, Francine turned, drew one of her six-shooters, aimed, and pulled the trigger. The bullet whizzed by several men and struck a vampire that was about to pounce. The vampire, a young man with sandy hair, looked stunned for a moment before dissolving into nothing.

"Bullets with holy water," Francine reminded the stunned crowd as she replaced her gun.

Hugo motioned to Watkins and pointed to a couple of lit lanterns brought by several of the townsfolk. Watkins retrieved the lanterns, giving one to Hugo and the other to Donavan.

"Close and seal the door. Whatever you do, don't open it until I give the word."

Watkins understood, and moved the crowd back. Hugo pulled out one of his crossbows and motioned to Donavan to follow. Francine pulled two knives out of her boots and brought up the rear. Once inside the barn, Francine waved to Watkins, who grabbed two men and shut the door. They placed a large board across the hooks and backed away.

The two lanterns barely penetrated the darkness. Hugo stretched out with his senses, searching for vampires. Francine walked towards the carriage, knives at the ready. The carriage door hung from one hinge, and Francine peered inside with her catlike eyes. Huddled in the corner of the carriage, the female stared out.

"Where's Donavan?" the vampire asked. "Did he bring us someone?"

"He's here," Francine said. "We brought no one."

"Need to feed. Need to feed," the vampire said, sounding desperate.

"Come out. We will take care of your needs," Francine said.

"You mean kill me?"

"If necessary," Francine answered.

"Oh, you won't be killing!" the vampire screamed, and leapt out of the carriage.

*

Hugo pushed the stench of rotting meat aside as he held up the lantern. He could hear Donavan whimpering in the dark. He closed his eyes and attuned his hearing. He heard a slight scratching above them. He raised the lantern above his head and in the gloom, he spotted the male vampire. He hissed at Hugo, who raised his crossbow.

Hugo fired just as he was struck from behind. The bolt smashed into the roof, but caused the vampire to let go of the beams. The lantern was knocked from his hand and landed on the ground, breaking open. The flames ignited the hay in the barn.

*

The female vampire flew out of the carriage and knocked Francine to the ground. She landed with a thud, but managed to scratch her assailant. Francine got to her feet in time to see her opponent strike Hugo from behind. As the hay caught fire, she glanced up to see the male vampire plummeting towards Donavan. She grabbed her six-shooter and fired.

*

Hugo turned and pointed his second crossbow at the female vampire, who was crouched behind the burning hay. She was hissing and looked up. Hugo turned to see the male vampire about to land on Donavan, but before he could react, he heard a gunshot. The vampire was struck in the head and exploded over Donavan, covering him in his filth.

Hugo was hit from the side and landed on his back. The female vampire was on top of him, her fangs aiming for his throat. His crossbow had landed a few feet away, and he was struggling to fight her off. Desperate, he brought up his knee and caught the vampire in the stomach. As she lurched up, Hugo grabbed a knife from his boot and rammed into the vampire's sternum.

Surprised, the vampire pushed off Hugo and got to her feet. Hugo leapt up and kicked the vampire in the chest, causing

146

her to fall backwards into the burning hay. As the flames consumed her, the silver knife finished the job, and she dissolved.

"Come on!" Francine yelled. Hugo turned and grabbed Donavan, who was choking on the dead vampire's waste. They ran to the door and cried out to Watkins to open it. Nothing happened. Francine cursed.

"Bastards going to let us burn with the barn," she spat.

Hugo looked around for another exit. There was none, and the rest of the barn was going up in flame. Francine glanced at Donavan. He was on his knees and choking. She pointed this out to Hugo.

"I think some of that vampire blood got into his throat. I think he's changing."

Hugo saw the change happening. He grabbed Donavan by the collar, dragging him to the carriage. Francine joined them, sheathing her knives. Donavan spat out blood and other fluids and looked at Hugo. The hunter saw the change, but he needed to feed to complete the journey.

"Donavan, use your hunger to help us. Let's ram this carriage into the door. There are lots of throats to feed on out there."

Donavan smiled and started to push the carriage; it moved very slowly. Hugo and Francine joined him.

"Find your power, Francine, we need everything!" Hugo yelled.

Both hunters reached within themselves. Years of hunting the dark forces had given them superior strength, but they needed to harness it. Hugo could feel the power rise. When it hit him, he called out to push.

"Now!"

The three of them shoved the carriage with everything they had and smashed through the door. The carriage flew out of the barn and across the street, landing on its side. Behind them, the ceiling collapsed, and the rest of the barn went up in flames. Watkins and the townsfolk were off to the side, staring at the wreckage.

Francine walked up to Watkins.

"Who refused to open the door? Who forced you to keep it closed?"

Watkins pointed to the man whose balls she'd grabbed earlier. She stormed up to the man, who was wearing a cocky grin, leapt into the air, spun around, and smashed the heel of her boot across his chin. The man gave a loud cry and fell to the ground. When she landed, Francine yelled to Watkins, "Tell Doc Elliot there's a broken jaw that needs fixing."

Hugo, bent over with his hands on his knees, looked up at Donavan. He was breathing hard and appeared desperate. "Thank you for helping us get out of there," Hugo said.

Donavan straightened. Shakily, he said, "I don't want to be a vampire."

Hugo nodded and pulled out his gun. Donavan shook his head.

"I'm not fully formed. Will the fire kill me?"

Hugo nodded once more, and Donavan smiled.

"Save my sister."

"We will," Hugo said.

Donavan turned to the crowd and said, "I'm sorry."

With that, Donavan walked towards the burning barn. When the flames engulfed him, he didn't cry out. Hugo watched as the barn burned down. Francine joined him and she held his hand.

*

At dawn, Watkins, the hunters, and several of the men finished scouring the town for other vampires. There were none. Of the dead, one was the town's mayor.

"I had wondered why he didn't show his face when you arrived," Watkins said to Hugo.

The townsfolk of Dead Bull gathered their dead, planned for the funerals, and discussed how to rebuild the barn. Hugo and Francine gathered their equipment, coats, and hats, and waited outside the sheriff's office for Watkins. When he arrived, he looked exhausted and rattled.

"We are grateful for your help, but I hope you understand that some of the folks here are a little bitter about what happened. They lost loved ones to outside forces and will be glad when you leave."

"No need to explain, Sheriff. We understand," Hugo said, and held out his hand which Watkins shook. Francine kissed Watkins on the cheek and smiled when he blushed.

"Get yourself a good woman, Sheriff; you need some looking after," she added.

Watkins returned the smile.

"What about Donavan's sister?" he asked.

"Top priority," Hugo said, picking up his sack.

Watkins watched the two hunters head for the station. He was still standing there a half-hour later when the train arrived. He breathed a sigh of relief when it departed.

A voice sounded behind him, and Watkins turned to see an apparition floating in the window next to his office. He gave a long sigh, then walked back inside. After he poured himself a large whiskey, he addressed the apparition which floated through the wall.

"It didn't seem right—after all they did—for us to ask them about our ghost problem, too."

After the Hunt

'What happens to the hunter when the hunting is done?'

Her mentor's words sounded in her head as she stepped into the shower. She groaned in relief as the hot water pounded her muscles. She stretched and twisted her neck and allowed the heat to do its job. She mulled the question in her head as she turned off the water.

"We will see in an hour."

Grabbing a large towel, she stepped out of the shower. The steam-filled bathroom obscured every glass surface as she dried off her tall and toned body. She pulled her reddish-grey hair into a long braid and hung the towel on the rack—a habit drilled into by her late mother.

The mansion was dark and quiet as she stepped out of the bathroom. Electric candelabras scarcely kept the dark at bay. She pulled a silk robe off the hook behind the door of the bedroom and wrapped it around her body. She paused at the mirror and took a long look, letting it linger. Her green eyes stared at the older, but still fit, warrior of the people.

The Huntress of monsters, she thought. *And now they come for her.*

Leaving the mirror, she stepped towards the window and spotted her immediate future: an angry mob led by men with forked tongues and poisonous lies. Torches and weapons were being wielded by the masses.

'They will see you as a threat, my dear Anna,' her mentor's voice came to her again. 'Remember Churchill.'

Anna allowed her thoughts to ramble back to her history books. Winston Churchill, who led England in their fight against the Nazis, was thrown to the wolves when the war was over. A warrior pushed aside when the fighting was done.

She snorted, turned from the window, and left the bedroom. Her footfalls echoed in the mansion as she headed down to her armoury. Her servants—two butlers, a cook, two maids, and a chauffeur—had all volunteered to stay and fight. She fought back tears at their loyalty.

After a long argument, however, she'd convinced them to go, giving them money and the keys to several safe houses around the country. That was two days ago, and she could still feel the warmth of their last embrace. She hoped with all her heart that they were safe.

"I will call for you when this is over," she'd said to them as they left. Now, the mansion held only memories of their comings and goings. Silence and sorrow hung in the air.

The stairs to the basement armoury were indented from frequent use. How many times had she commented to her head butler about replacing them? She pushed the thought away as she heard the mob approach the fence.

Might be nothing left to replace if this mob has its way.

As she approached the armoury door, a small sign on the wall caught her attention:

**To protect the innocent,
One must sacrifice innocence.**

The sign was a reminder of the duty she performed. She thought of the first creature she had dispatched: a werewolf preying on the children of a small village. She was sixteen, and it took everything she had to win the battle. As the life left the creature's eyes, she felt a piece of her go with it.

"It strips away your humanity," her Mentor had said at the time. "That is the price we pay for taking a life, regardless of the fact that it's justified."

She opened the armoury door and disrobed. As she donned her gear, she wondered how many of the creatures she had dispatched were innocent. Just outcasts, or following their nature. She remembered a strange cat-woman from years ago. All she wanted was to be left in peace, but she was persecuted. The town paid Anna's fee. The cat-woman paid Anna with the memory of her dying eyes.

"The sum of her life was a few lousy coins in a pouch," Anna muttered, as she pulled on her Kevlar top and gloves. She coldly shoved the thought away as she adjusted her boots. When the light in the room dimmed, she smiled.

Ah, they found the electric fence. That will hold them for a bit.

She selected two short swords and sheathed them on her back. Knives were tucked into her boots. A couple of shotguns and other small daggers were placed strategically around her body. She stretched and moved her limbs, testing the suit and her mobility. Satisfied, she turned off the lights and locked the armory door.

As she walked up the stairs, she hardened herself for the fight by remembering a job she did in the Himalayas. She had been hunting the Yeti, and allowed herself to be kidnapped by the cult that worshipped the creature.

The six cult members brought her to a cave in the mountains during a blizzard. They secured her with ropes and gagged her. When finished, the members, blinded by their faith in the creature, knelt and closed their eyes to pray. Anna waited a few moments, then easily freed herself. She pulled the hidden knives out of her boots and waited for the creature.

The creature had put up a spirited fight, but, in the end, had succumbed to her skills and fortitude. She threw its severed head at the praying members who, alarmed at the death of the creature, ran out of the cave and into the blizzard.

Anna chuckled as she stepped into the main floor of the mansion. She had stayed in the cave for three days. She built a fire, skinned the creature, ate its flesh, and used its hide to stay warm. When she emerged from the cave, she walked by the corpses of the cult members, their faces frozen in agony, as she made her way back to their hut to collect her weapons.

The voices of the mob outside her door tore her from her memories. She drew the swords from her back and adopted a position close to the door, stretching her limbs and focusing her body and mind. She glanced at the paintings on the walls. The figures stared at her, witnesses to the coming fight.

She took a deep breath as the mob hammered at the door. She thought about the leaders of the mob, cowards playing chess by throwing the pawns at her first. She would savour their deaths when the time came. As the doors splintered under the pressure, her mentor's voice came to her:

'In the end, Anna, once all the monsters have been hunted, the people will fear no longer—and their jealous leaders will come for you.'

As the door broke free, Anna adopted her fighting stance. The mob stared at her for a moment before charging forward with a collective roar.

Let them come.

The Last Train

Canadian wastelands, Feb 2060

"One ticket, please," Percy Locke said.

Behind the bars of the station booth, a face etched with the signs of death stared back him. As the old man collected the fare and printed off the ticket, Percy wondered what drove this man to continue to come to work. His infection would kill him within a matter of days. Perhaps coming to work, despite his impending death, gave him a purpose. Not that the paycheque would mean anything, with the last of the uninfected leaving. After today, everyone in this sector would be dead within two weeks. Percy shuddered at the thought.

"Your ticket and change," the old man said.

Percy took his change and ticket. He thanked the old man, who just waved him off and called to the next person in line. Percy made his way to a wooden bench and sat down. Staring at the lineup, Percy noticed two young women holding hands, one with dark hair, the other red. They were dressed in old-style jeans, and long-sleeved shirts, one displaying a classic rock band named 'Rush' that Percy didn't recognize.

Behind them was a bald black man and his small Asian wife. He was dressed the same as Percy, formal suit and tie, while she wore a traditional Chinese robe and wide hat. They all carried winter coats but no luggage, for fear of contamination.

They brought only what they wore, things which had been already decontaminated.

Percy glanced beyond the lobby to a large window. On the other side of the glass stood an elfin woman wearing a black body suit and parka. She smiled at him, and he waved back. She nodded and turned away while Percy rubbed his left shoulder instinctively. He remembered the shot and her words:

"Remember Percy. You must make it."

Percy steeled himself, and ran over his instructions again.

"I can't fail," he thought.

"Last train to Moose Jaw arriving," a tired-sounding voice announced over the speaker system.

Percy headed to the door leading to the tracks. Taking one last look around, he stepped out of the station.

The platform had been cleared of snow, and salted. Despite the heavy parka he wore, the cold wind bit into him. The young women were huddled together, while the bald man sheltered his wife from the wind. A whistle caught Percy's attention, and he turned.

The old steam train pulled into the station, coming to a stop with a large hiss. The train was pulling six cars. Percy and the others would be getting on the fifth. On top of each car were two men stationed by large pulse rifles mounted to the roofs. Percy shuddered at the sight. A large man wearing a yellow insulated suit with a transparent face plate came up to the five passengers.

"All aboard, everyone. I will brief you inside."

Percy allowed the others to board first. He stepped up into the car and turned left, facing the rows of seating. He sat down in the first seat, while the two young women made for the back. The bald man and his wife were seated in the middle. The yellow-suited man pulled the door shut and pushed a couple of buttons on a side panel. A hissing sound shot through the air. He took off his helmet and turned towards the passengers.

"We're sealed in, folks. No getting off until we get to Moose Jaw," the man said, pulling out a small tablet. "Now for your briefing. My name is Dawson, and I will be looking after you on this trip. On board we have: Percy Locke, Mr. and Mrs. Elijah Thompson, Stacy Robarts, and Margaret Turning."

After acknowledgement of names, Dawson continued.

"Alright. Bathrooms are at the back, and I will be serving you some decontaminated food in a bit. We have one more stop to make, and then on to MJ for Decon. From there, you will be flown by Military transport to the Manitoulin Island research facility. Once processed, you will be sent either to the Atlantic Provinces or to Australia. They are the only free zones currently accepting people."

Dawson paused, awaiting questions. There were none.

Dawson punched a button on his console, and the sound of the whistle could be heard. The train lurched forward and pulled away from the station. Percy glanced out the window and saw the old ticket counter attendant staring at the train. He wondered if the old man would live out his last days or end it himself sooner. Percy pushed the thought away as the platform gave way to the endless drifts of snow on the prairies.

The soup was bland but hot. Percy wondered if he could detect a chicken flavour but wasn't sure. As he sipped his soup, Percy thought about the tattoo on his left shoulder. It was of the Greek God Hermes, the messenger.

"Once you are being processed in Moose Jaw, the doctors will see this image and you will be separated," Dr. Yale had said, coughing into her gloved hand. "The new facility was moved to North Twin Island in Hudson Bay. It was the most remote but accessible place. Your blood will be extracted and hopefully synthesized into a cure."

Percy remembered Dr. Yale's pleasant manner, and missed her. Seeing her standing outside the station was a surprise but one he welcomed, even though they didn't dare speak. He wondered how long the lab would be able to keep her alive.

Percy pushed the thought away and sat back in his chair. He combed his blond hair with his fingers and rubbed his eyes.

So much riding on one man, he thought. *There have to be others out there who have found the link.*

His thoughts were interrupted by a voice behind him.

"Mr. Dawson. Where is our next stop? I was under the impression that Swift Current was quarantined."

Percy swivelled in his seat to face the voice. It was Elijah Johnson.

"It's just an outpost, about twenty klicks outside of Swift Current," Dawson answered. "It will be a quick stop—only three people."

"Only three people left?" Percy asked. "Is that all?"

Dawson turned and gave a sad smile.

"Yes, and it will be a quick stop. We have reason to believe that a large group of Infected is in the area. They may try to board the train."

Percy nodded at the answer, got up, and strolled down the aisle to Elijah. Dawson passed him, touching the big man's shoulder on his way towards the back to check on the young girls. Percy extended his hand and introduced himself.

"Pleasure," Elijah said, taking Percy's hand. This is my wife, Yue."

Percy shook Yue's hand. She smiled and shyly looked away.

"I was teaching English in Beijing when the infections happened," Elijah said.

Percy didn't need to hear anymore. The Chinese government blamed the infection on foreigners. In the span of two weeks all non-Chinese people were deported—even naturalized immigrants. Shockingly, Beijing fell only a week later.

"Yue and I were living together. When I was deported back to Vancouver, she decided to come with me," Elijah continued.

"What did you do for a living, Mr. Locke?" Yue asked.

Percy paused and thought to himself, *How much do I tell?* He decided on the truth.

"I worked at the University Lab, studying the infection," he answered, unconsciously rubbing his arm. "When the evacuation order was given, I was the only one not infected."

"So, you must know about the effects and how to stop them," said a voice from the back.

Percy and the Thompsons turned to see one of the young women standing in the aisle at the back. Her long black hair was pulled into a ponytail.

"I only know what everyone else knows," Percy said, keeping the main secret from them. "I have no idea what will happen when we get to Moose Jaw. Hopefully, we all get on that plane."

"Stacy, we are going to get on that plane, right?" the redhead, Margaret, now standing, asked her friend.

Stacy took Margaret's hand in hers and kissed her lightly on the cheek. Stacy whispered into Margaret's ear, which brought a smile to the woman's face.

"We'll be on that plane," Percy said, despite knowing that it might not be true. "We'll be on that plane."

*

The frozen wasteland passed by Percy's window as the train rumbled on. Silence filled the car except for the soft murmurings of sleep from the Thompsons, and quiet moans from the girls in the back. Percy smiled sadly at his reflection in the window. Even at the end, these people had each other and wouldn't be alone. He wasn't so lucky.

Percy was a confirmed and fervent bachelor. His life was his work. No time for partners or friendship. He counted beakers and microscopes as his companions. Dr. Yale was the closest thing he'd had to a human friend in years. He thought of his parents, who he rarely saw. The boarding schools were a cesspool of bullying and harassment. Percy's schoolwork was the only thing that got him through it.

Percy's woolgathering was interrupted by the slowing of the train. Dawson came out of his little office in the front of the car and walked up to Percy.

"Last stop. Must close the blast windows."

The others stirred at the lack of motion. Percy caught a glimpse of the small station, and the three people clad in parkas waiting inside, before the windows went black.

"What the hell is happening?" Margaret shouted, leaping from her seat.

"We are picking up the last of the uninfected," Dawson answered. "We should only be stopped for a couple of moments."

At that, the train came to a complete stop. Percy could feel the hairs rise on the back of his neck. Dawson went to his communication terminal and listened. A voice confirmed boarding, and the train slowly pulled away. Relief filled the car as Percy noticed the Thompsons, now awake, wearing concerned faces.

Dawson smiled as the train picked up speed. The smile was short-lived, as panicked voices came over the speaker followed by the sound of blasts firing from the pulse rifles overhead. Percy and the others joined Dawson at the front, Stacy and Margaret hugging each other, Yue holding Elijah's hand.

The train thudded but stayed on the tracks. More firing, and for the first time, cries of pain and terror from outside the train. Voices over the speaker sputtered words:

"Hundreds of them…came out of the snow…barrier broken through."

Percy's mind was racing as he pictured the scene of infected people trying to stop and board the train. His eyes welled up. He rubbed his shoulder, knowing that it was too late for these poor souls.

More voices came over the speaker and Dawson turned to his charges.

"All clear. I think we could all use a drink."

The five passengers agreed as they took their seats. Dawson hit a button, and the blast windows slid back up into place, revealing a horrifying sight.

Dead bodies were strewn over the landscape. Many were without proper clothing, and most looked frostbitten. A scream came from the back. The group turned to see Stacy pointing at the back door.

Through the window, a young woman was staring in. Her hair was mostly fallen out and she was frostbitten. Her cracked lips made noiseless pleas to be let inside. Margaret pulled Stacy back as Dawson pressed a button on his console.

Percy looked on in terror as the woman reached out, only to be shot several times from the roof. Percy got to the window in time to see the woman fall off the train and into the snow.

Stacy was crying as Margaret held her. Elijah walked with Dawson to the back door. Dawson pushed a couple of buttons on the back console and breathed a sigh of relief.

"No contamination," he said, as he looked to the floor and then to the passengers. "I'm so sorry."

Elijah put his hand on Dawson's shoulder. Soon the entire group were ensnarled in a group hug, which they held for a long time.

It was night when the train pulled into the Moose Jaw decontamination centre. The powerful lights illuminated the giant concrete structure. As the train stopped, Dawson addressed the group:

"Last stop. When the door opens, you will be guided to the Decon area. It has been an absolute pleasure."

An alarm sounded and the train door opened. Percy waited until the others had departed before exiting the train.

The group was led into a large, tented area where they were instructed to strip off all clothing and enter the showers. An hour later, wearing white robes, they were ushered into a room where a group of doctors examined them, and took blood and other vitals. A First Nations woman was poking and prodding Percy when she pulled the robe away and noticed the tattoo.

She gave Percy a strange look, then walked to a console, punched a button and spoke into it. The others in the room were now staring at Percy. Soon, a small man, with large glasses, dressed like the other doctors, came into the room and glanced at the tattoo. He sighed, and said to Percy in a quiet voice, "You're too late. The North Twin Island facility was infected. It's lost."

"But Doctor Yale said that this vaccine would cure the infection," Percy said.

The small doctor picked up a syringe of Percy's blood, squeezing a few drops into a portable scanner. A few seconds later, the results scrawled across the small screen. The Doctor sighed again.

"Was Doctor Yale in good health when you last saw her?"

"Yes, I believe so," Percy answered.

"Well, you might as well know, we received a message from North Twin before it went under. It seems Doctor Yale sent infected people to the facility under the guise of the safety tattoo. I'm sorry Percy, but you're infected as well."

Percy's face went white. He looked over at the others, who were now being led into another wing. Margaret looked backed, smiled, and turned away.

"They're all fine. You're not at the contagious stage yet. They will be on the flight to Manitoulin within the hour. We will be leaving soon after."

Two hours later, Percy watched the last plane leave Moose Jaw. In that time, he was informed that Doctor Yale had already expired from the infection, and her reasons for spreading the virus remained a mystery.

He was now alone in the facility. A loudspeaker echoed through the building with a countdown to an explosion to sterilize the area. Percy walked outside and gazed at the last train. He admired its lines and strength. Tears filled his eyes, not because of Dr. Yale's betrayal, but of the peace the survivors would spread. He heard the last count, the klaxons—and then nothing.

Four Ghosts and a Funeral

Bobby Brake put the car in Park and examined himself in the rearview mirror. He looked and felt like shit. Digging a comb out of his pocket, Bobby struggled to make himself presentable. His bloodshot eyes and unshaven face would betray his night of debauchery, but at least his hair would look alright.

Sighing, Bobby dragged himself out of the car, shut the door, and leaned against it. He looked around the church parking lot, searching for anyone who would give him a hard time. His consensus: everyone in sight.

Bobby smoothed out his black suit, took a pack of cigarettes out of his jacket pocket and lit one. He was about to take a second drag when he heard a familiar voice from behind.

"Booby Brake, you S.O.B.! How the hell are you?"

"Don't call me Booby!" Bobby said, as he turned around.

"Booby! Booby! Booby!" Jack Thomas yelled in a mocking voice. He slapped Bobby on the shoulder and continued, "I honestly didn't think you were going to show up."

Bobby looked at his schoolyard chum. Jack was well-polished and looking great. Even with his hair turning slightly grey, old Jack was a stunner.

"I didn't think I was going to show up either. However, Mom gave me a call. You should have heard the guilt trip she sent me on. I had to pack an extra bag."

Jack took in Bobby's appearance and shook his head. "You have a rough night?"

"It was like sandpaper," Bobby answered. "Honestly Jack, I don't know why I came. I haven't seen my cousin Ellie in over twenty years. We weren't that close."

"Well, there was that one time. . ." Jack said.

"Listen to me," Bobby snapped, taking a last puff on his smoke and crushing it out. "I don't care what the rumours are, it isn't true. I swear I will beat the hell out of anyone who says otherwise."

"Who-says-what otherwise?" a familiar voice from behind asked.

Turning, Bobby and Jack stared at Mona Parsons. She looked like she'd stepped out of a fashion magazine.

"Jack, my love, you are looking fine. Which is more than I can say for you, Bob. You look like you just crawled out of a trash can."

Bobby couldn't take his eyes off Mona. At six-feet-tall, dressed in a black suit with high black boots and her blond hair tucked up under a wide-brimmed hat, the woman possessed the most amazing superpower—causing erections. Bobby remembered her from school. Every time she got up to leave math class, she turned the classroom into a camp site with all the tent poles being erected.

"Well, Mona, I *have* had a rough couple of nights," Bobby said.

"More like a rough couple of decades. I'm surprised you're here. I mean, with that *incident.*"

"Nothing happened, OK? Why is this so hard for you to understand?"

Mona stared at Bobby. Bobby closed his eyes and took a deep breath. When he opened them, he was staring directly into Mona's big blue eyes. His mouth dropped opened.

"Well Jack, it's great to see you," Mona said to Jack. To Bobby, she said, "Bobby, close that mouth of yours or I will slap them drooling chops off your face."

Bobby closed his mouth as Mona walked away towards the church. Jack slapped Bobby on the back.

"See you inside," he said smiling, and followed Mona.

Bobby hung his head and sucked up his courage. He was about to start off when he spotted another familiar face. Wally 'The Weasel' McMurphy was walking along the side of the church. Bobby raced over to Wally and cornered him by the wall.

"Wease, my buddy. You gotta help me out. Whatcha got on ya?"

Weasel, the unfortunate but accurate nickname for Walter McMurphy, was the town's tow truck driver and local dealer in shitty drugs. Bobby got into Wally's face with a desperate look on his own.

"Wease, I can't go in there without a little bit of help. You got to believe me—there are people inside who would feed me to their dogs."

"Does it have anything to do with what happened with your cousin?" Wally asked.

"*Nothing fucking happened,*" Bobby hissed in a low, annoyed voice. He calmed himself and continued, "I will take anything you got."

Wally sighed and resigned himself to fate. He reached into his jacket pocket and pulled out a small packet.

"It's not what you think, but it's all I have." He put it in Bobby's hand with a small smile on his face.

"Thanks, old man," Bobby said, as he ripped open the package and swallowed the two pills. They tasted sweet. "How much?"

"On the house, seeing it's your cousin's funeral."

Bobby patted Wally on the shoulder and turned away. He got to the walkway in front of the church, and with an effort, took a deep breath and walked inside.

*

The church itself was typical for a small town in Newfoundland. Situated on the hill overlooking the community, it was mid-sized and could hold about a hundred people on a good Sunday. For Ellie's funeral, however, the place was packed, with extra chairs put out.

As he walked up the aisle between the pews towards the casket, Bobby could hear the whispers of those seated. He glanced up at the figures on the stained-glass windows and could feel their scornful stares. He was relieved when he reached the closed casket with Ellie's picture placed on top in a pewter frame.

Ellie's brown eyes stared out of the picture and drilled holes through Bobby's spine. He leaned towards the picture and spoke.

"Ellie, I am so sorry you're gone, but what the hell did you tell everyone about that night?"

A collective "Shhh" came from the front row. Bobby turned to see his mother and his Aunt June staring daggers at him. Bobby nodded and walked towards the left side of the church, avoiding eye contact with everyone. He spotted Mona sitting with Jack. She wore a smirk on her face.

Bobby found an empty chair and quickly sat in it. He leaned forward and put his head in his hands. He was sweating, and hoped Wally's pills would kick in soon. He let out a long breath and was about to sit up when he heard a familiar voice behind him.

"Really stepped in it, didn't you?"

Bobby recognized the voice of his Uncle Frank. He shook his head before answering.

"Jesus, Uncle Frank, nothing happened."

"I'm not talking about that. How could you break your mother's heart by coming back here after what you did?"

"That wasn't my fault. The investment fell through. We all lost money."

"She nearly lost her house. Your cousin Peter lost his business. You were a fool to get involved with that investment."

"Listen, you old coot," Bobby said in an angry whisper as he turned in his seat. To his surprise, he was staring at a young boy sucking on a lollipop. A confused look appeared on Bobby's face as the boy pointed at him and laughed.

"Shhh," came from the boy's mother. Bobby put up his hand and turned around to face the front. He could feel the stares on his back. He lowered his head, rubbed his eyes, and decided that the pills were kicking in. It also dawned on him that his Uncle Frank had died three years ago.

"I'm glad you didn't attend my funeral, you loser," Frank's voice rang in his ears.

Bobby snapped up with his fist raised. He caught the eye of the priest, who was stepping up to the pulpit. Bobby lowered his fist and placed his hands on his lap. The priest raised his eyebrows, before turning to the mourners.

"Welcome, everyone, to the celebration of life for our poor Ellie Masters, who was taken from us far too soon."

Bobby tuned out the welcoming speech and rubbed his eyes again. He felt his heart racing.

What the hell did Wease give me? he thought. He should be feeling calm at this point, but instead, he was sweating bullets. He wiped his eyes and tried to get the image of Ellie out of his head.

"Let us stand and sing our first song of the service: 'I'll Fly Away'," the priest announced.

Attendees rising out of the pews filled the church with their collective grunts and groans. Bobby struggled to his feet as he reached out and grabbed a Hymnal. He opened it to the index to find the song but didn't see it. A large hand slapped him in the chest. Bobby looked up to see a large man holding the program of the service against him.

"Thanks," Bobby whispered, as the man quickly turned away and carried on singing.

Ellie's face stared back at him, her large brown eyes bordered by her long brown hair. In the picture, she was wearing a black turtleneck sweater with jeans. It was taken in front of the lighthouse at Lobster Cove Head just outside Rocky Harbour. Suddenly, he felt aroused, and immediately regretted it.

A surge in the singing brought him back, and Bobby hurriedly looked inside the program for the words to the hymn. It took him a second to find his place and he opened his mouth to sing.

Bobby could feel the eyes upon him. Usually he was a good singer, but the morning after a bender, all he could muster was a croaking sound, like a frog in heat. He stopped singing and mouthed the words.

When the guitar player, an older man named Carlson, played the last note, the priest took a long look at Bobby before carrying on.

"You may be seated. I would like to ask Jack Thomas to come forward and read Psalm 23."

Jack stood up and smoothed out his suit. Bobby could see the ladies undressing Jack with their eyes as he walked to the front. He stepped up and stood next to Ellie's picture.

"It's an honour to be here. Ellie was my good friend, and a beautiful soul."

Bobby scoffed. Ellie hated Jack's guts. The only reason he was here was because he used to suck up to Aunt June when he was a kid.

"Sure, I will have another cookie, Mrs. Masters. This is some nice house, Mrs. Masters. You look lovely in that shirt, Mrs. Masters."

It made Bobby sick. If he hadn't known better, Bobby could have sworn that Jack wanted to sleep with his Aunt June. Jack finished up the Psalm and smiled at everyone as he took his seat. Bobby wanted to take the bastard out back and give Jack's dentist some work.

"Now, everyone, please stand as we sing, 'It is Well with my Soul'," the Priest said.

As Bobby stood, he felt the call of nature. The Blue Star beers he'd had last night were coming back to haunt him. As everyone started to sing, Bobby quietly retired to the back of the church where the washrooms were located. He figured he had at least four minutes to finish his business and get back.

As he entered the bathroom, Bobby recognized a familiar odour. Someone was smoking pot. He got down on his hands and knees and looked under the stalls. He saw a pair of legs. He got up, strode over to the stall door, and kicked it in.

Wally dropped the spliff as he reeled back from the door. Bobby reached in, grabbed him, and hauled him out of the stall.

"What the hell did you give me?" Bobby asked, as he pulled Wally close to him. "I should be tripping right now instead sweating my ass off."

Before Wally could answer, a voice from the other end of the bathroom called out to them.

"Bob, let him go. He hasn't done anything to you that you haven't done to yourself."

Bobby turned to see his dad standing there. He closed his eyes, chose his words carefully, and replied to his father, "Dad, stay the hell out of this. You've no right to say anything to me."

"Who the hell are you talking to?" Wally asked.

"My Dad. You know, who drank himself to an early grave and left Mom with nothing? The prick is standing right over there."

Bobby gestured, but the bathroom was empty. Wally pulled himself away and went to the sink. Bobby was still staring at the spot where he'd seen his father. When he finished washing his hands, Wally walked up to Bobby.

"I didn't give you anything you couldn't handle, but if you're seeing your dead dad, maybe you should lay off the stuff you were already on."

Bobby said nothing as he continued to stare at the spot. Wally shook his head and walked out of the bathroom. It took

Bobby a minute to realize that Wally had left, and to remember the reason why he was in the bathroom in the first place. He walked into Wally's stall and relieved himself.

What the hell, he thought. *First Uncle Frank, now my dad. Jesus, what's going on?*

As he was finishing, Bobby heard the door open, and then footsteps. He zipped up his fly, exited the stall, and headed to the sinks. Standing in the middle of the bathroom was Danny O'Brien, local insurance agent.

"Alright, Danny?" Bobby asked, as he turned on the water.

Danny was sniffing the air. Bobby stared at him through the mirror.

What the hell is he sniffing? Bobby thought, remembering Wally's burning spliff behind the toilet. He closed his eyes and leaned his head against the mirror.

"Are you smoking dope in here?" Danny asked. "You are, aren't you?"

Bobby turned to Danny, his hands splayed out.

"Danny, look man, it wasn't me. I just came in to take a piss."

"You're taking a piss, alright," Danny said. "It's bad enough you came back for this funeral, but now you're smoking dope in a church. What the hell is wrong with you?"

Bobby opened his mouth to reply and thought better of it. He walked past Danny and out of the bathroom. The singing had stopped, and the priest was welcoming Mona up to the front.

Mona turned towards the crowd and smiled. Bobby nearly dropped to his knees. Mona looked radiant, and he felt queasy. As he moved carefully along the side of the church to his seat, Mona started her eulogy.

"Oh, my dearest Ellie. You were such a loving soul."

Bobby scoffed. *Some loving soul,* he thought. At that moment, he spotted a familiar face leaning against the wall next to him. Paul Watkins, his beat-around buddy from years ago.

"Rumour was she stole from the residents of the local nursing home. It was never proved," Paul whispered.

"The kindness she showed for others, and the charity work she did for the community," Mona continued.

"You mean the charity of Ellie Masters."

Bobby chuckled to himself as Paul continued, "Funny how some of that money always ended up in her pockets. She was a piece of work."

"Her legacy is her enormous heart and love for her family." Mona summed up her eulogy, wiping a tear with her handkerchief. She smiled at the congregation. Before she departed the pulpit, she whispered in the priest's ear. He nodded as he watched Mona take her seat next to Jack.

"I'm sure the priest is glad he's wearing robes at this point," Paul said, and Bobby laughed out loud.

The priest shot Bobby a look as Bobby put a hand over his mouth to stifle the laughter. He could also feel the stares of the rest of the congregation. He glanced at his mother, who wore a look of shame.

Bobby turned back to Paul. He was surprised to see that he had left. He turned in his seat to see where Paul had gone but couldn't spot him.

"All rise as we sing 'Amazing Grace'," the priest said.

Bobby stood and mouthed the words. The voices of the faithful echoed around the church as they belted out the lyrics. Bobby felt himself getting caught up in the moment. The words resonated within him, and he felt remorse. Not just for Ellie, but for all the other shitty things he'd done in his life.

He glanced down at the program and saw that the service was almost finished. A few words from the priest, another song, and out the door. He was relieved that it was almost over.

I can hit the road to St. John's and be back in time for happy hour, he thought.

As the song wound down, Bobby took his seat and rubbed his forehead.

Bloody pills. Should've kicked in by now. No matter, he would get something on the way back.

"Now, as we bring this service to a close, it was suggested to me that instead of a message from me, that Bobby Brake would like to say something about Ellie," the priest said.

Bobby nearly fell out of his seat. He collected himself and stood up. As he walked to the front, he felt his stomach start to churn. The congregation practically threw contempt at him as he gazed out at them from the front. He straightened his tie and took a deep breath.

"What can I say about Ellie that already hasn't been said?" he started. "She was beautiful, and a great cousin."

A rap from behind startled Bobby. He turned to see the closed casket. He ignored it, turning back to the congregation.

"She was my friend, and we hung out a lot back in the day—" Another rap from inside the coffin threw him off. He looked back at it. Nothing. He spotted the priest, who was giving him a puzzled look. He kept going.

"We, well, spent a lot of time together." Another rap. "Jesus Christ!" Bobby yelled, startling the congregation. He approached the coffin and put his ear to it. He heard Paul's voice.

"I don't think she can hear you."

Bobby raised his head and gave a slight laugh. *I'm losing it,* he thought. As he walked back to the pulpit, he felt his eye twitching. He looked over the crowd and saw confusion. He kept going:

"We would talk about life and our place in it." Behind him, Bobby heard the coffin open. He spun around to see Ellie sitting up and giving him an evil smile.

"Holy shit!" Bobby yelled. "Ellie!"

The congregation, stunned by this outburst, started to whisper to themselves. Bobby closed his eyes. When he opened them again, the coffin was closed. He turned and, to his horror, he saw Ellie standing in the aisle. She was still smiling at him.

"Tell us what happened that night," Paul's voice sounded in the church.

"Why don't *you* tell them, Paul," Bobby yelled. "It's not like you weren't there."

"I knew it!" a voice screamed from the front. It was Aunt June. "You bastard! You had sex with her!"

The congregation gasped. Bobby was stunned as he watched his mother grab June and tried to hold her back. Jack had his phone out, filming the whole thing. Mona was sitting there, smirking.

Bobby's eyes darted in every direction. Everyone was yelling at him—or at other people. It was chaos. He turned back to Ellie. To his shock, he saw that standing beside her were his dad, his Uncle Frank, and Paul.

A hand on his shoulder brought him back to reality. The priest was standing next to him, wearing a sad look on his face. Bobby pushed the priest's hand away and yelled at the crowd.

"I didn't have sex with her!"

The congregation stood silently. "Yes, I wanted to, and we fooled around but, I couldn't do it."

"What was that?" Mona's voice shouted from the back.

Bobby glared at her. "I said, I couldn't do it! I—I mean, we, we…we got to a certain place, but I—"

"Needed Viagra!" Jack yelled out, still filming the event.

Laughter erupted in the church. Bobby lost control of himself. "Why don't you ask Paul Watkins! He's standing right there!" Bobby pointed to the empty aisle.

"Paul Watkins died three years ago, you ponce." It was Wally who was speaking. "You didn't even come home for your good buddy's funeral."

Bobby shook with rage. He spotted Wally at the back, leapt off the pulpit, and raced down the aisle. He punched Wally square in the jaw, and the Weasel fell to the floor. Bobby was on top of him, throwing haymakers.

"You son of a bitch! What the hell did you give me?"

It took several people to pull Bobby off the Weasel. As he was held in place, June ran up and punched Bobby several times in the face. His mother joined in. The priest called for calm, Jack continued to film, and Mona stood by, licking her lips.

An hour later, Bobby was in a straightjacket, jabbering about seeing dead people as he was loaded into an ambulance. He spotted Mona standing with Jack as they watched the footage on his phone. Bobby saw Mona taking hold of Jack's hand while she grabbed his ass with the other.

Bobby also saw his mother consoling Aunt June, and the police talking to Wally. As the paramedics closed the door, Ellie appeared next to him in the ambulance. She was smiling and pointing to his groin. Bobby closed his eyes and passed out.

As the ambulance pulled away, the police continued to talk to Wally.

"I swear officer, I only gave him sugar pills.

Orlanda

Orlanda Stevens lay in the hospital bed in a coma. She had no idea that her family had been killed in a car accident, and that she was the only survivor. She also didn't know that the person who hit them was drunk, and driving with a suspended license. He lay in the hospital bed across from her.

Orlanda stirred as sunlight infiltrated her eyelids. She opened her eyes and looked around the room. The right-hand side of the room was intact, while the left side resembled the bombed-out ruins of buildings in Syria.

As she sat up, Orlanda was able to look out past the ruined walls into a desert landscape. Standing next to the wall was a man. He was balding, and wearing a set of white overalls. He was waving to her to come forward.

Orlanda groaned as she slid out of the bed. The floor was cold on her bare feet. She stood up, letting the hospital gown fall to her knees. She fumbled with the ties at the back as she walked towards the man. Once at the ruined wall, Orlanda gazed up at the man and recognized him.

"Uncle Kevin?" The old man nodded. "What are you doing here?"

Kevin smiled before answering.

"I'm glad you remember me. I have been away a long time."

Orlanda shook her head. In the back of her mind, a memory screamed to be heard. She ignored it.

"What's going on? Where am I?"

Kevin smiled again, sadly this time, and pointed back into the room. Orlanda turned and was shocked to see her body lying in the bed, tubes and electrodes attached to her. Kevin said, "You've been in an accident."

*

"Loser. You were always such a loser."

Thomas McKay gazed down at his hands as his father berated him. He sat in a chair overlooking the desert. In front of him, Jimmy McKay, a tall and fearsome Scotsman, continued his barrage of insults.

"Did I not teach you anything?"

"No, you were too busy being drunk," Thomas said, finding the courage.

"Don't you turn this back on me. I've paid my price, and you're looking to do the same if you don't do exactly what I tell you."

"Do what exactly?" Thomas asked.

"Fight."

*

"What accident?"

Kevin hesitated before answering. "A drunk driver hit you."

"How? I mean, I'm seventeen, but Dad never lets me take the car out by myself."

"Trust me, that's all you need to know right now," Kevin said. "Come along."

Kevin led Orlanda away from the ruined walls towards a small junk pile. When they got closer, Orlanda recognized several things from her childhood. Her beaten-up bike, her old bow and arrow set, as well as the replica Spartan helmet she got after seeing the movie *300*.

She picked up the helmet, put it on her head, and asked Kevin, "Where the hell am I?"

*

"Fight?" Thomas asked. "What the heck is this place?"

Jimmy lost his patience with his son and grabbed him by the scruff of his neck. He pulled Thomas out of the chair and dragged towards a ruined wall. When Thomas looked around the side of it, he saw himself in an isolated hospital bed. There was nothing else around him.

"Fight for your life," Jimmy continued. "That's why you're here. You have a chance to wake up."

Thomas stared at himself in the bed. He turned his gaze to his surroundings, but there was nothing but hard sand.

"I'm dead?" he asked.

"No, but barely alive," Jimmy answered.

Anger rose up inside Thomas. He spat on the ground and turned back to his father, who was smiling.

"Who the hell did this to me?"

*

"I don't know what it's called, but it's a place that allows you a chance of survival."

"You mean, I'm not dead," Orlanda stated.

"Not yet, but you have a chance."

"Why are you here?" she asked, picking up her old baseball bat.

"When these challenges happen, those involved are allowed an advisor. Someone related or close to you to guide you. In this case it's me."

"Why?"

"It just is. It's never explained," Kevin answered.

Orlanda gazed down at the junk. She looked back at Kevin.

"That is the sum of your life up until now. With this, you must make a suit of armour."

*

"*You* did," Jimmy answered. "Got wasted and drove into a family just outside Otherville."

"What the hell was I doing there?" Thomas asked. "That town gives me the creeps."

"Doesn't matter why you were there. You're here now," Jimmy said, pointing to a wrecked car just past a small dune. "Now, get over there and prepare yourself."

*

Still wearing the helmet, Orlanda picked up the bow and arrow, removed the bike tires, and, using some old rope, tied them together, slipping them over her head to make a front and back shield. Next, gloves, knee, and shin pads from her skateboarding days, and a pair of old steel-toed boots her dad made her wear when she helped him with chores.

"You were always a tomboy, Orlanda," Kevin said. "You were swinging a hammer before you ever picked up a doll."

Orlanda smiled. She finished off by picking up a toy sword and shield with a maple leaf on the front of each one.

"Ok, I think I'm ready."

Kevin gave her a sad smile and motioned for her to follow him.

*

Thomas stood in front of the wreckage and, using his instincts, closed his eyes. Parts of the wreckage flew off the ground and encased his body. Thomas felt emboldened in his new armour and turned to Jimmy. The old man was smiling.

"Now, that you're ready, let's head to the arena."

"Arena?" Thomas asked.

*

"The arena is where you will fight for your life," Kevin said. "Hence the makeshift armour."

Orlanda looked down at herself and wondered if she'd made the right choices—not that she had much to choose from.

Kevin led the way across the dunes. In the distance, Orlanda saw a shiny city with tall buildings. To the left of it was an enormous dark pit. Before she asked, Kevin spoke.

"The city on the right is a place of peace. The pit, a place of punishment. How it works is like this. If you are decent in life—place of peace. If you were questionable, you have a chance to stay in the place of peace, but you must face a challenge. If you were a complete…" Kevin trailed off. He paused for a moment before finishing. "If you weren't a nice person, into the pit with you."

Orlanda frowned and gazed up at Kevin. Suddenly, she was back in her home, watching her dad scream at Uncle Kevin. The bruised face of her Aunt Shirley was stained with tears. Orlanda looked up at the present Kevin. He just nodded.

"I'm in the pit."

*

Thomas strolled towards the arena and saw the long line of warriors. He turned to Jimmy, who said, "The battles are endless. We shall have to wait our turn."

Lined up in front of Thomas were some of the most brutish-looking people he had ever seen. Men, women, animals—it didn't matter. All if them had a quarrel with someone, and they looked ready. Thomas took inspiration from the lot and turned to Jimmy.

"Piece of cake."

*

"Didn't Aunt Shirley forgive you?" Orlanda asked.

"She did, but she still kicked me out. Don't get me wrong, Orlanda, I deserved it. Stupid me though, I kept drinking and ended up killing myself by stumbling in front of a truck."

"Sad way to die," Orlanda said.

"It sure is."

"Didn't Shirley's forgiveness help you in the afterlife?"

"No. Forgiveness only helps the one wronged. It gives them a sense of peace and the strength to deal with the pain. That fact that Shirley forgave me doesn't mean I don't get punished."

Orlanda walked in silence for a bit. Before she could ask, Kevin cut her off. "Don't ask about the pit."

*

Thomas heard the cheers from the crowd. He turned to Jimmy, who remained stoic. The line was getting shorter, and Thomas was growing impatient.

"Listen to those cheers. I am going to make you so proud of me."

Jimmy nodded, but wore a grim look on his face. "You had better pull this off, otherwise…"

"Otherwise, nothing, Dad. I can already feel the beer running down my throat."

Jimmy grabbed Thomas and spun him around.

"You stupid idiot! Don't be daft! Remember what happened to me. I promise you son, if you keep this shit up, you are going to end up in the same place I am—and believe me, you don't want to be there."

Thomas grinned, shoved Jimmy back, and snarled, "You don't get to give me any advice! You beat me, you son of a bitch! You died in a shoot-out with the cops trying to rob a bank. You left us with nothing! Mom drank herself to death and it's your fault! So, you don't get to give me any advice!"

Jimmy stood back and shook his head.

"I know I made a ton of mistakes, but you've got to believe me. You don't want to end up…"

"Screw you, old man. Just go back to your hole and leave this to me!"

Jimmy gave Thomas a sad smile and turned away. Thomas blinked, and the old man was gone. He was stunned at the suddenness of it. As he felt a tinge of sadness for Jimmy, Thomas heard the cheers of the stadium and he quickly forgot the old man.

"Bring it on! I want to live!"

*

The large building appeared out of the haze. To Orlanda, it seemed the building was growing. She also noticed a long line of people waiting to get in. As they got closer, Orlanda realized the people in line looked sad and very haggard.

"What is this place?"

"It has no name. It's a holding place for all the wrongfully killed."

"Wrongfully killed?" Orlanda asked. "What does that mean?"

"People murdered, or killed by any other criminal acts. Collateral damage, or anything else like that. They must stay there until the perpetrators themselves have died. It's a sad place."

Orlanda stared at the people in the line. They stared off in space as they shuffled along. She felt a tug on her arm as Kevin tried to guide her away. She was about to go with him when she spotted someone she knew.

"Mom!" she shouted, and pulled away from Kevin. Orlanda ran towards her mom and hugged her. The woman stared blankly and didn't return the gesture. Kevin put his hand on Orlanda's shoulder.

"She doesn't know you, lass," he spoke. "She has the eternal sadness."

Orlanda squeezed her mother harder and closed her eyes. Kevin finally managed to pull her away. Her mom just kept shuffling along. Orlanda started to cry as she watched her go.

"Come on," Kevin said.

Orlanda slowly started to turn when she saw her dad, with her sister Kara walking behind him. She called out, but they didn't acknowledge her either. Kevin gently tugged on her arm again, but she refused to go. She kept shouting at them, but they kept shuffling along like her mother. She waited until the three of them were inside the building before dropping to her knees and crying.

Kevin knelt next to his niece, holding her. Orlanda buried her head into his chest, sobbing. Kevin glanced up at the line as it continued to move along. It seemed endless. Eventually, Orlanda pulled away and wiped her eyes. She stood up, adjusted her helmet, and looked at Kevin as he got to his feet.

"Who did that to them?" she asked, barely getting the words out.

"Your opponent." Kevin answered.

Orlanda said nothing as Kevin led her away from the building. Seconds later, she heard cheering coming from a large arena. It reminded her of the Roman Colosseum. Kevin brought her to a side entrance, where there was a shorter line. The cheering became louder, and Orlanda gripped her sword tighter.

"Why?" she asked.

"Why what?" Kevin asked back.

"Why did this person kill my family?"

Kevin looked down at Orlanda and shrugged.

"I don't know."

Orlanda nodded slightly. The line continued to shrink, until they found themselves next to enter the arena. When she inquired about the speed of the line, Kevin simply answered, "Time moves differently here."

*

Thomas strolled into the arena with his fist raised. He spun around as he walked, taking in the atmosphere. He did a little dance for the crowd, pretending he was a cocky boxer ready to destroy his opponent.

As he confidently walked to the centre of the arena, the far doors opened and out strolled a young girl dressed as a bicycle. Thomas roared with laughter as he spotted her helmet and toy sword.

"This will be a massacre!" he screamed to the crowd, who roared their approval. "I can already taste that beer."

*

Orlanda and Kevin waited patiently until the door opened, and a strange-looking creature let them in. They stood in a long hallway with a closed door at the far end. Orlanda was shaking with fear and anger. She looked up at Kevin, who was looking nervous.

"Who is in the crowd?" she asked.

"The damned," Kevin answered. "Every now and then, the pit allows these sorry souls to sit and cheer on the carnage. Think of it this way. The righteous have a harder hill to climb than the weak and sinister."

"How do you know that?" she asked.

"I've sat in those seats and cheered," Kevin answered. "You don't know what the pit is like; anytime you can get away, you get away."

Orlanda looked at her uncle, and saw the fear and exhaustion in his face. She couldn't imagine what horrors he'd witnessed—or experienced himself.

"Don't get me wrong, Orlanda; I deserve to be there, so don't be feeling sorry for me." He paused as the far door opened.

"Now listen to me. To win or survive this you need to remember—your family is gone. You can't save them. So, to keep their memory and love alive, you put it here." Kevin pointed at Orlanda's chest. "Now, to fight this guy, you need to put your hatred away. He will taunt you, but don't fall for it. The only way to beat him is to use your head and his arrogance against him. Don't fight for anyone else but yourself."

"Not even you?" Orlanda asked.

"Especially not me. Now, fight with your head, not your heart, and finally, do you remember all those times you helped your dad fix the family car?"

Orlanda nodded. Kevin touched his nose with his finger and smiled. "Go get him," he added, and lovingly smacked her helmet.

Orlanda punched Kevin in the chest, drew her sword, adjusted her shield, and walked to the end of the hallway. At the door, she turned and looked at Kevin one last time. He gave her a thumbs-up as she walked into the arena.

*

"Little girl, little girl. Did something happen to your family?" Thomas yelled, to the delight of the crowd.

Orlanda strode forward with her head held high. When she got within ten feet of Thomas, she stopped, adopted a fighting stance, and glared at him. In the back of her mind, the voice of Gurney Halleck—a character from one her favourite books, *Dune*—came to mind.

Thanks Gurney, Orlanda thought. *Not a direct quote but good enough.*

Orlanda spied Thomas's evil grin and ignored it. His armour was shaped like a car, but really, it was as if Thomas had turned the car over on its top and was laying on the undercarriage. His arms and legs were protected by the tires, and the brake lines held them in place. One of the car doors protected his torso, and its window retracted to allow Thomas to speak. Orlanda recognized the car as a Volkswagen Bug. It made Thomas look like an overgrown turtle.

"Have you been a good girl in life?" Thomas taunted as they started to circle each other. "It's the pit for you if you haven't. You can smell it from here."

Orlanda had smelled the pit when she walked into the arena. She ignored it, and with a sudden lunge, slashed Thomas across the knee. Thomas grunted and stepped back. Orlanda noticed how he stumbled around. His outer shell was a little cumbersome.

"Is that the best you got?" Thomas yelled, as he stepped forward. Orlanda took a couple of steps back as Thomas lashed out with his tire-covered fist. She lifted her shield, but the force knocked her back. Orlanda fell onto her back but quickly recovered.

"Is that the best *you* got?" she yelled back at him, knowing that he'd nearly knocked the wind out of her.

Thomas laughed and flicked his arms. The tires covering his hands started to rotate. Soon, they were spinning so fast that the tires started to hum. He stumbled forward again and swung his right tire. It hit her shield with such force that it nearly took her arm off. Orlanda ran a few steps and turned back.

"I'm going to laugh at your dead body when I wake up!" Thomas yelled. "In fact, if I get the chance, I will spit in your face!"

Laughter erupted from the stands. Thomas ran forward swinging his right tire. Orlanda slashed at it with her sword, only to have the sword ripped from her hands and broken in two. Thomas swung the tire with a backhand, but Orlanda ducked and scurried away. As she steadied herself and raised her shield with both hands, Kevin's words about working on cars came back to her.

She noticed that Thomas's power was still be provided by the car's engine. A plan quickly formed, and she adopted a fighting stance. Thomas laughed as he stumbled towards her. He swung his right tire at her, but she ducked, dropped her shield, and jumped onto his arm as he fell. She grabbed the brake line and pulled it off. As Thomas started to rise, she leapt to the other arm and did the same. She jumped to the ground as regained his footing.

"Stupid girl," Thomas said, when he saw what Orlanda had done. "Just because I can't use the brakes doesn't help you—in fact, it could ruin you."

Orlanda ignored him and picked up her shield. She motioned him towards her, and the big man stumbled forward.

She backed up towards the broken sword, picking up the hilt and throwing it at Thomas's head. The faceplate window rolled up and the hilt bounced off. Thomas lowered the window again and laughed.

Orlanda steadied herself as Thomas lashed out with both hands, falling on her back as the tires ground into her shield. She could see his sinister grin as he pushed down. Orlanda waited just a moment more before sliding under the shield, and then shot her foot upwards, catching Thomas between the legs.

Orlanda rolled out of the way just in time to see the tires slam Thomas in the bits. He roared in pain as he lifted his hands, and instinctively moved them towards his private parts.

As he bent over, Orlanda ran around the back and popped the latch for the hood of the engine. She grabbed every wire and plug she could find, including the ones on the battery terminals. The power in the car died, leaving Thomas was stuck in a half-bent position.

Orlanda strode confidently around the frame and took off her helmet. Thomas, who couldn't move, snarled at her. She pointed at the car window in the down position and smiled. Thomas gaped at Orlanda as she hauled off and smashed Thomas in the face with her helmet.

Thomas's bloody and dazed face looked back at her. Orlanda stepped away from Thomas, whose armour released him, and he fell to the ground, defeated.

The cheering in the stands went silent. As Orlanda stretched, a tall figure dressed in black appeared in front of her. A voice emitted from its dark hood.

"You will live; your family will be released and moved to the city. One question, however: Do you forgive him?"

Orlanda looked down at the ground. Behind her, Thomas had gotten to his feet and spotted her shield. He walked over, picked it up, and headed towards Orlanda.

The figure waited a moment before Orlanda answered. "I…" she said, and after a pause continued, " . . .forgive him."

The figure nodded as Thomas came up from behind and raised the shield. Before he could strike, Orlanda added, "That doesn't mean, however, that he shouldn't be punished."

A hidden force grabbed Thomas just as he was about to attack. He flew out of the arena and out of sight. Orlanda glanced up at the figure, but found herself falling backwards. She fell for a few seconds before her surroundings changed and she landed in her hospital bed. Her body ached, and she pulled at the tubes in her arms.

Hands held her down on the bed and she heard a familiar voice.

"Sweetie, oh sweetie, don't move."

Orlanda looked up to see her Aunt Shirley. She was crying.

"They're gone. They're all gone," Orlanda cried out, as the tears streamed down her face. Shirley leaned in and hugged her. Behind them, a doctor at another bed was turning off a defibrillator.

"He's gone."

Orlanda closed her eyes and let the grief engulf her.

Two months later, Orlanda stood in front of the graves of her family. She still needed a cane, but the bruises on her face were gone, and the cast on her arm was about to come off. She cried some more, and eventually turned away.

She didn't tell Shirley about Kevin; her aunt didn't need to know. In her heart, she had forgiven him—that was enough. She didn't tell anyone about her time in the coma either. She convinced herself it was a dream, and she could live with that. She knew her family was free of that awful building.

"They're still alive in your heart." That was Kevin's message. Basically, keep living. She smiled, said goodbye to her family, and walked out of the Otherville graveyard towards her Aunt Shirley, who was waiting for her.

The Subconscious Always Rings A Lot

"What the hell is going on?" Martin asked, as he leaned back against the rock face.

He was panting, and the breeze from the mountains offered no relief from the sweat that poured down his face. He gazed down and gasped. The drop was endless. He closed his eyes, hugging the rock face.

"Deep breaths, deep breaths." he repeated to himself. Slowly, he regained control. He opened his eyes again and stared into the distance. He only saw wisps of clouds and treetops.

"How did I get here?"

"The same way you always do." A voice came from above. Martin looked up and watched his ex-wife float down to him. "You always did stupid things and got yourself into weird situations."

Martin groaned, and felt his patience run away from him.

"What the hell are you doing here, and how the hell are you floating?" he asked.

"It's your stupid dream," she replied, now floating in front of his face. Her fierce blue eyes boring into him. "You can't even have nice dreams like regular people."

"I can't help who I am." Martin said, leaning into the rock face.

"Yes, you can!" she yelled. "Why do you have to do everything differently? My dad warned me about you."

"What do you mean, 'warned you about me'?"

"He said, 'Bella, there's something off about the lad. He's not like us'."

"What's wrong with being different?"

"You don't do regular things. You can't play sports. You're not handy. I asked you to paint the bedroom and you made an absolute mess of it. You can't swing a hammer to save your life. You're useless."

Martin slowly tapped his forehead against the rock face. Bella's shrill voice hurt his ears. He decided to push back. He noticed that Bella was wearing her leopard print dress. It made her look like a prostitute.

"I see you're still dressed for walking the streets. Pick up any tricks lately?"

Rage filled Bella's eyes, and she let out a roar. Martin continued, "All those nights you worked late at the office for Mr. Donavon. Your knees must be sore from working on that promotion."

"Rotten little bastard!" Bella screamed. Obscenities filled Martin's ears as she screeched at him. Finally, he'd had enough and pushed off the rockface.

"Bye Bella, and to hell with you."

Bella screamed at him as he fell away from her. The trees rose up around him as he braced for impact and slammed into the ground. Everything hurt as he rolled to his side. He gazed up at the trees and saw a large fern. Confused, he looked around and found himself on the floor of his apartment.

"What the hell?"

Looking up, Martin noticed an empty light socket, an overturned stool, and a broken light bulb on the floor. He rolled onto his back, and his memory supplied the answer. His stomach was hurting, and the antacids hadn't given him any relief. He was in the middle of changing the lightbulb when his head took him to the cliff.

"What the hell did I eat?"

He got to his knees and used the ladder to regain his footing. He felt dizzy and was sweating. He stumbled around the living room, and found the broom and dustpan. When he bent over to pick up the glass, he nearly fell over again.

"I have to lie down."

He abandoned the glass and headed to the bedroom, leaning against the walls as he walked. When he reached the bedroom, he sighed and launched himself onto the white bedspread. As he fell, however, the white sheet turned to a blanket of clouds. Martin cursed as he turned in the air and glanced up at the plane he'd just fallen out of.

"Christ Jesus!"

He instinctively flailed his arms. He was spinning as he fell, his view switching from the sky to the ground, the latter approaching at great speed. He glanced down at himself and noticed he was wearing a harness. He laughed out loud when he saw the rip cord.

"Alright! Here we go!" he yelled and yanked the cord. Nothing happened.

Martin frantically pulled on the cord repeatedly. Still, nothing. He glanced down at the fast-approaching earth and gave it one last tug. The cord caught and the parachute released.

Martin watched as the white silk unfolded above him. The chute caught and jerked him upright, the harness ramming his balls into his stomach as it tightened around him. As he tried to control his nausea, Martin noticed that the parachute hadn't slowed his progress. In fact, he was descending at a faster rate.

He looked up at the chute. It was torn, and had a gaping hole in the middle. Martin cursed and closed his eyes as the ground came up to meet him.

"Shit!"

He hit the floor with a thud. Dazed, Martin opened his eyes and found himself on his bedroom floor. He was wrapped up in his bedsheet. He groaned, unravelled himself, and tried to sit up. His back and knees protested. He wiped the sweat from his forehead and let out a long, deep breath.

"What in the name of god was that?"

"I'll give you 'What in the name of god was that?'!"

Martin turned to see his old drill instructor, Sergeant Grant, looking down at him.

"On your feet, you little piece of garbage!"

Martin leapt to his feet and found himself in an army barracks, wearing a poorly pressed uniform. Looking out a window, he saw the sign for Canadian Forces Base Cornwallis: Basic Training Headquarters.

"Oh no," Martin said to himself, as Grant started to berate him.

"Connors, you're useless! A grubby little shit-addled prick who can't even shine his own boots! What the hell are you doing here?"

Martin wondered the same thing. Grant's face was two inches in front of him as he continued:

"I've seen blind monkeys in wheelchairs who were more useful than you! You're as useless as a snake's armpit! At least my epileptic dog could still dig a hole when he was having a seizure, if you held him the right way!"

Martin flinched as Grant's spittle caught him in the face. The Drill Sergeant's menacing eyes and bald head reflected the fluorescent lights of the barracks. His immaculate uniform and starched creases were sharp enough to slice bread. He glanced down at the railway tracks on the front of Martin's pants and shook his head.

"Stop wasting your time, Sergeant. He won't listen to you."

Martin recognized the voice. It was his dad's.

"Oh no," Martin said again, which earned him a mean look from Grant.

Martin's dad, old Richter Connors: a lean, chain-smoking, hard-drinking womanizer who lectured Martin on just about everything growing up.

"You listen to me because I'm an expert in this," Richter used to say. Martin knew better. The man was an idiot, but when you were a kid, it was listen to the lecture or have it beat into you.

"Dad, what are you doing here?" Martin asked.

"Shut your filthy cake hole, you poor excuse for pond scum!" Grant yelled, as his face turned red.

"Didn't listen to me," Richter said, shaking his head. "Now look at you. You're such a failure that even your subconscious is yelling at you."

Martin glanced at Richter.

What did he mean by that? he thought. Grant continued his tirade.

"You dumbass little dirtbag! Now you're deaf too? You're slimy, rotten, egg-smelling, vomit-inducing, turd coloured…!"

Martin and Richter watched in horror as Grant convulsed and burst apart. His head torpedoed itself to the ceiling and attached itself to one of the beams. It was still yelling at Martin. Grant's body flailed, and his arms elongated. He looked like one of those inflatable tube men at a used car dealership. One of the arms swung out and smashed into Richter, sending him sailing through one of the windows.

Martin shook himself and ran from the scene. Grant's arm caught him in the back, and he grunted as he hit the floor. He rolled over to see Grant's body, now holding his head, crawling towards him. The head was still yelling, but making incomprehensible guttural noises. As it reached out to grab him, Martin shut his eyes.

Martin felt the carpet against his face and opened his eyes once again. He was back in his house. Picking himself up, Martin looked at the overturned shelf with his DVD collection. Staring up at him was his copy of John Carpenter's "The Thing". He sighed and went to the bathroom to wash his face.

The cool water felt good. Martin glanced at his reflection. Bloodshot eyes sunken into a pale unshaven face. Martin sat down on the side of the tub and held his head in his hands. He felt like shit.

As he sat there, Richter's words came to him. His own subconscious yelling at him. Martin had fallen on hard times after the military.

"You can only go overseas so much before it affects you," his counsellor told him.

Martin felt nauseous. As he lifted the toilet lid, a voice came from the bathroom door.

"Your father's right, you know."

Martin looked up to see his mother standing there. She was petite, and wearing her favourite red dress and shoes. Her hair was perfectly coiffed. She was shaking her head.

"What do you mean 'he was right'? He was an idiot."

"In this case only," his mother said. "He was a bastard and treated us poorly, but he *is* right."

"Dad's been gone for ten years," Martin said as he stood up. The bathroom had transformed into his childhood bedroom, and he was wearing his Spiderman pjs.

"Do you think this is real?" his mother asked. "It's all in your mind. I'm not here. You're not in your bedroom, and why did you picture yourself in those pjs?"

Looking sheepish, Martin answered, "They were my favourites."

"I know. You wore them so often that in the end they stood up by themselves."

Sighing, Martin sat down on his bed with the Star Wars quilt. He shook his head.

"Help me."

"I can't. I'm not here. Why don't you visit me?"

"She's right. Why don't you visit her?"

Martin looked to his right to see Richter staring at him.

"Because he's stupid and doesn't do things like regular people!" Bella yelled. Martin looked up to see her flat against the ceiling.

"Loser! Loser! Loser! Press your pants properly!"

Martin turned to see the Sergeant Grant Thing crawl through the window. He closed his eyes and yelled, "Stop!"

He fell back on the bed. When his head hit the pillow, instead of a soft landing, he heard a 'clunk' and passed out.

*

Martin awoke in the tub. As he stared at the shower curtain, tears rolled down his face. He struggled to get up, and found that he had made a mess of himself. After he undressed, Martin took a long, hot shower. As the water seeped into his muscles, his situation seeped into his thoughts.

Had he been hiding? The world at times seemed too much for him. He had buried himself amongst the things that made him happy. Crawled inside the eggshell and curled up. Well, maybe it was time to crack the shell and get back to living.

When he finished his shower and shaved, Martin noticed that it was four in the morning. He got dressed, cleaned up the glass, and straightened out the DVD shelf. He made coffee, poured himself a cup, and took the steaming brew outside to his small patio. The cool air refreshed him.

He resolved to visit his mother. It was only a three-hour drive. It would be good for the two of them, even if he only stayed for a few minutes. That was probably all he could take, but it would be a start.

He also thought of the cashier at the grocery store. She seemed interested. Why not ask her out? Coffee could be a welcome invitation.

He noticed his hands shaking. He clenched his fists, and the shaking stopped. He took a deep breath and smiled.

"One step at a time, old buddy, one step at a time."

In the back of his mind, Martin could hear Richter saying, "This is going to be good for you, boy. I know—I'm an expert on this."

"Fuck off, Dad," Martin said, shaking his head. "Just fuck off."

The Last Xanadu

The far future

The cold, biting wind tore at her hood as she encouraged the dogs to push on. With their destination in sight, the woman allowed a small smile to stretch her cracked lips. Ignoring the pain and blood, she shouted gleefully at the dogs, who picked up on her excitement and raced up the final hill.

The entrance to their destination was a small cave that would have been missed by a casual glance. The driver, however, had the eyes of a cat, and spotted the depression in the rock wall at once. She halted the dogs and stepped off the sled.

Pulling dried meat treats from her pockets, the driver glanced at the empty traces and gave a quick prayer to the brave dogs who didn't make it. She unhooked the remaining three and gave them the treats. The huskies ate greedily and rolled around in the snow. Laughing, the driver knelt and gave each a well-deserved belly rub.

After attending to the dogs, who were now lying in the snow, panting happily, the driver stood up and removed a small flask from underneath her parka, taking a drink. Refreshed, she put away the flask and walked towards the entrance. Once inside and out of the wind, she produced an ancient parchment and studied it. Satisfied of the location, the driver went out, secured the sled, and removed her belongings. Calling to the dogs, the driver entered the cave.

She was immediately attacked by the smell and the warmth. Pulling her hood back, the driver closed her eyes and breathed in the distinct aromas of a long-forgotten greenhouse. Opening her eyes, the driver was overcome by the depth and colour of the landscape.

As she walked among the flowers and fruits, the dogs followed. After scaling a low hill, they came upon a small waterfall, fed by a river that disappeared into the rocks above them.

"Alph," she said, as she looked up at the domed ceiling which allowed light to enrich the plants. She walked along a path that led to another brightly-lit room. Sunbeams of dust illuminated the furniture, which had only one purpose: pleasure and comfort. The driver smiled. Whistling to the dogs, who were drinking from the river, she took off her parka. Following the directions on the parchment, she started her chores.

Hours later, the driver, carrying a tray of honeydew melon, jars of oils, and candles, ascended a stairway towards another cave entrance. Wearing silk robes, her feet bare, the driver shivered slightly as she entered the dwelling lined with ice and snow. Forcing the cold away, the driver walked purposefully towards the centre of the large room.

The man was naked, enclosed in a glass box, sitting in the lotus position, and supported by a wide chair,. The driver lay the tray down and opened the door of the box. She lit the candles, allowing their aromas to fill the box, awakening the man. With her hands coated in the oils, the driver slowly applied them to the man's muscles. The combined effect of candles and oil brought him around.

His breathing and heartrate, which had been almost non-existent, exploded with rhythm and noise. He slowly opened his eyes and gazed upon the driver. Her Eurasian face smiled back at him. He reached out and touched the long black hair, her bold green eyes inviting him.

She leaned in and whispered into his ear, "The First Reign of Men is over. It is time for you to return and guide the Second Rise."

"How long have I slept?" he asked in the ancient tongue.

"My Lord Khan, it has been centuries. Many things have happened to the world you sought refuge from," she answered.

She fed him the melon, which he ate slowly. Satisfied at his strength, she pulled him forward and helped him stand. Khan leaned on her, and she supported him, despite the fact that he towered over her. She led him to the pleasure room, where an enormous fire from beneath the mountain lit the space, and gently laid him on the freshly-made bed. Khan gasped as she allowed her robe to fall from her body. He gasped again as she engaged in the lovemaking.

*

Khan gazed into the fire as he lay in the bed. Basking in the afterglow of their joining, he pulled his thoughts together. Immortality was both a gift and a curse. The days of his self-exile were lost to him, a side effect of the long sleep. He looked around the room, his 'pleasure dome' as they called it.

Feeling his movement, she asked, "Is anything wrong, my lord?"

"Tell me again why I was awoken?" he asked.

"The ancient text by your hand demanded that, at the Fall of Man, you were to be brought back to lead the survivors. They need a saviour, a new messiah."

Khan turned, and was possessed by her eyes. He lost his questions as he lost himself in her. Hours later, Khan stood staring out at the landscape, at the great wall silent in the moonlight, a sentinel constantly on guard. She was next to him wrapped in a fur; he was still naked. Questions raced through his mind.

"What is beyond our lands?"

"Relics. Relics of machines and monuments that you cannot comprehend. The men lost control of themselves and, in the end, the natural world fought back. Their Xanadu was a dream. Though they built many castles and fortresses in search of it, it was an illusion. An idea that they could conquer the Earth with no consequences. Warnings were ignored so the pursuit of wealth and power could proceed unhindered. When it was too late, their collective shock reverberated for generations."

Khan continued to stare out at the stars. Her words sank into him, and he shuddered.

"How do you know I would be any better? My memories are lost to me, but at your words, I feel the guilt of my actions in my bones. Immortality has not made me better; it has only prolonged my own savagery."

"I do not understand, my lord. The parchment, written in your hand, has guided and inspired us since you imprisoned yourself. Why do you forsake your own words?"

Khan left her side and wandered towards the ancient river. Alph continued its flow from its unknown source. Even after centuries, the river still flowed, unchanged. Khan sensed this, in him and in the future. He turned back towards the driver.

"I forsake my words because I have not changed. I will be as ruthless as those you described, because I must be. In the end, I will be pushed aside by others who think they are stronger. There is no change, just more of the same."

He walked over to her and noticed the tears. He wiped them away and spoke:

"I know this is heartbreaking for you. Your mission to wake me has been a dream for you—a lifetime of preparation. I am sorry, but I must say no. Let the world heal itself. From what you have told me, let the world of men discover new things without the aid of some old dictator."

The driver looked up at him and found comfort in his words. Nodding, she took his hand and led him back to the bed. He allowed her to control everything; she was magical.

*

After a full day of preparations, Khan sat in his box again, slowing his heartrate and breathing. The driver, satisfied with his state, closed the door and stared at him for a moment before departing. She strode through the gardens, and reaching the entrance, turned to gaze back at Khan's paradise. She donned her parka and whistled to the dogs.

Outside the cave entrance, the driver loaded her new supplies, hooked the dogs up to the sled, and took up her position. Before she signaled the dogs, she let Khan's words sink into.

Let the world heal itself.

She took a deep breath, a last look around, and signalled the dogs. As they raced down the side of the mountain, she wondered if burning the parchment was a good idea. She remembered his words about men discovering new things. Let them make their own way here and discover this last Xanadu.

The Moai Barrier

London, England, January 1842

Queen Victoria sat upon her throne overlooking her court and sighed at the number of people who demanded her attention that day. The cold wet air in the building forced the Queen and many of her subjects to wear furs, or at least heavy coats. Many were stifling sneezes and coughs. The overall atmosphere put the Queen in a sour mood.

At the end of the day, and the court dismissed, Prince Albert, the Queen's husband, walked up to the throne and whispered to her that an urgent private audience was requested from one of her sea captains. When she inquired, Albert impressed on her to allow the meeting. The Queen sighed again but smiled for her Albert. After a moment, she permitted the audience.

Albert motioned to the guards, and a harried man with a tattered naval uniform, long hair, and beard strode in with an uneasy but purposeful gait. The click of his boot heels echoed in the chamber. The Queen sat up on her throne and gazed down at the unkempt man with knotted eyebrows.

"One of *my* captains?" she asked Albert without turning.

"Yes, your Highness," he answered.

The man stopped in front of the throne and bowed. The Queen sat back and, with a quick wave of her hand, motioned the man to speak. He nodded and began.

"Your Highness, my name is Captain Phileas Armstrong of the HMS Northern Star."

"Your appearance disputes that, Captain Armstrong," the Queen said dryly.

"I know, your Highness," Armstrong said. "But my information, I believe, will more than make up for my appearance."

The Queen glanced at Albert, who said nothing. After a moment she nodded for Armstrong to continue.

"My Queen, I have seen a wonder that would strengthen the Empire and bring all of our enemies to their knees."

"Well?" the Queen asked impatiently. "Where is this wonder?"

"Easter Island, your Majesty," Armstrong replied. "Our ship stopped there to make repairs after some bad weather. It was there that we witnessed this wonder."

The Queen turned back to Albert who nodded.

"Well, regale us, Captain, but I warn you, this had better not be a waste of the Queen's time."

Armstrong nodded and began his tale.

*

"Longboat's secured, Sir. All ready to take you ashore," First Mate Holden announced as Captain Armstrong exited his cabin and made for the port side.

"It's all yours, Holden. Be quick about the repairs. I would like to be on our way at the nearest possible time," Armstrong said, as he got into the boat.

Armstrong stared out at the sandy beach as the boat was lowered into the water. Further up the beach was a huge gathering of the local natives. They wore traditional clothing, and were chanting and playing small drums. Many of the women, Armstrong noticed, were clutching red pieces of wood.

Armstrong kept his eye on the group as his two crewmen rowed for the shore. Once close enough, the two men jumped out and pulled the boat up the beach. Armstrong stepped out and looked around.

The natives paid no attention to him and carried on with their ceremony. Armstrong scoffed and turned to face his ship.

"Savages," he said to himself.

"Oi, Sir. Look!" one of the crewmen said.

Armstrong turned around to see a man running down the beach towards them. He was a small but well-built man, balding, and wore the clothes of an Englishman. Armstrong gave his crewmen a puzzled look and marched forward to meet the stranger.

"Good day, Captain," the man called, as he neared Armstrong, who was a foot taller. "Welcome to Easter Island or, as the locals call it, Rapa Nui."

"Easter Island will do," Armstrong said. "What is your name and how did you arrive here?"

"John Nullius. I was left here under the orders of Captain Beechey in 1832 to learn what I could about the culture. I hope to write the narrative of this visit for future generations of Englishmen. I am a teacher by trade."

"Nullius? Strange name for an Englishman," Armstrong remarked.

"Indeed," replied Nullius. "I believe my father came from Greece, but I was born in London."

Armstrong looked beyond Nullius, and watched the ceremony for a moment. He shook his head.

"May I inquire as to your being here, Sir?" Nullius asked.

"My ship, the Northern Star, is headed to Australia, carrying prisoners sentenced to transportation. We were hit by a storm off Chile and stopped here to render repairs."

"But why come this way?" Nullius asked. "I would have thought it shorter to come around Africa."

"True, but at the last moment we were ordered to deliver goods and special documents to St. John's, Newfoundland. Afterwards, we sailed down the coast of the Americas and ended up here."

Nullius nodded as the ceremony behind him picked up in tempo. Armstrong turned away and walked down the beach, the teacher following. After a bit, he turned and asked Nullius.

"Alright, what are they doing?"

"They are preparing for the Rongorongo Festival, or the Reading of the Tablets. It is the most important gathering of the inhabitants. It is how Nga'ara wrestled control from the Birdmen who once ruled Rupa Nui."

"They still look like a bunch of savages to me, but at least they are not as bad as those aboriginals in Australia," Armstrong said. "They make the Indians in Canada look like Englishmen."

Nullius opened his mouth to speak, but kept it to himself. Armstrong noticed it and thought to himself, *He's gone native. I won't have him on my ship, even if he asks. I can't wait to get back to England and be among my own people.*

As they walked, Armstrong noticed the enormous stone heads on the hills. He wondered what would possess the natives to carve and mount these statues. He put the thought out of his mind when Nullius asked, "My dear Captain, the locals are planning a feast for this evening. Would you join us?"

Armstrong thought he would rather drown than attend such a gathering. He looked at Nullius and pitied him. Yet, against his better judgement, he agreed. Nullius clapped his hands.

"Excellent! I will inform the locals of your attendance."

As Nullius ran off, Armstrong turned to one of his oarsmen.

"Get back to the ship and tell Holden to hurry up with the repairs. I don't want to be here a moment longer than I must."

*

The feast that evening proved satisfactory to Armstrong, given his prejudices. Nullius seemed to be in his element, conversing with the locals and explaining to Armstrong the stories of the Rongorongo Festival. Armstrong nodded when he had to, and tried to ignore the other events of the evening.

As the feast was winding down, Armstrong longed for his cabin and his whiskey. He bid Nullius to join him as he walked to the shore. In the dusk, Armstrong noticed the giant statues, which Nullius called the 'Moai', standing like sentinels overlooking the ocean. He got a weird feeling as he walked by them; it was as though they were looking at him. He shook it off as he reached the beach and his longboat.

"Nullius, I am hoping to be leaving as soon as the repairs to the ship are complete. If you have any papers or letters to be sent to England, please have them ready by morning."

"Thank you, Captain," Nullius replied. "I will have something for you in the morning."

With that, Nullius turned and left the beach. Armstrong boarded his longboat, and soon was drinking whiskey in his cabin. Holden was seated across from him.

"I will be honest, Sir, those statues give me a strange feeling."

Armstrong sipped his whiskey and longed for England.

224

In the morning, Armstrong ordered Holden to take a longboat ashore to gather some supplies and meet Nullius. During the night, Armstrong had had vivid nightmares about storms, and the destruction of ships. He took a shot of whiskey along with his ablutions and walked out onto the deck.

The Second Mate reported that the prisoners had been fed, and the repairs completed. Two hours later Holden returned with supplies and a package from Nullius.

"Reports and some letters," he spoke. "Looks like the beggar was up all night."

"Fine. When we are a few miles away, throw the lot overboard. I don't believe there is anything of value to be reported from this place."

As Holden turned to give orders of departure, a loud rumbling could be heard in the distance. Confused looks ran through the crew as they searched for the source. A second rumbling was reported a few minutes later.

Armstrong turned to look out over the ocean. He saw nothing but water. He turned back to the shore and saw the locals, along with Nullius, standing just off the beach, also staring out towards the water.

The Northern Star bounced up and down from the wake of the unknown sound. He was about to give the order to weigh anchor when Armstrong noticed the beach. The water was receding at a rapid pace. He turned to Holden.

"Tidal wave."

Holden's face went white. Armstrong shook himself and bellowed, "Tidal wave! Secure the ship!"

The crew stood stunned for a moment before running in all directions and shouting. Cries from the prisoners below, who had heard Armstrong mention the tidal wave, pleaded for mercy and release. Armstrong stared at the ocean. He couldn't see the wave but knew it was coming. He ordered the anchor up and said to Holden, "Turn the ship into the wave. It's our only chance."

Holden ran to the quarterdeck and grabbed the wheel. The receding water which pulled the ship away from the shore gave her some momentum. The ship slowly revolved, but Armstrong felt it wouldn't be enough.

He turned back to the island and saw a strange sight. The locals were standing still instead of heading for cover. Even Nullius stood there. He was about to look away when he saw the statues moving. Armstrong wiped his eyes and stared again. The large statues were pulling themselves out of the ground and standing up.

Armstrong stared incredulously as the statues strode down to the beach and lined themselves up about thirty feet into the water. They raised their arms to the sky and stood still.

"Captain! The wave! We're not going to make it!"

With that, the wave rose and smashed into the ship. It was lifted and carried towards the shore. The crew and prisoners cried out, and Armstrong fell to the deck. He readied himself for the worst when the ship came to a violent stop.

Armstrong got up and ran to the starboard side. The ship was being held up in the air, caught by the statues. The water shot through the spaces between the stone giants and splashed harmlessly against the shore. The crew was speechless.

As the water began to flow naturally once more, the giants lowered the ship down into the water. Armstrong stared at the statues as they slowly turned around and walked towards the beach.

"What the hell was that?" Holden asked, joining Armstrong at the starboard side.

Armstrong shook his head. As the giants returned to their resting places, Armstrong noticed Nullius on the shore. In a fit of passion, Armstrong walked over, grabbed the teacher's package, and threw it to him. It landed in the water. Nullius waded out and retrieved it.

"I hope you never leave this island!" he shouted to Nullius. "This whole island is cursed, along with you and your friends!"

Nullius looked stunned as the ship floated out to sea. Armstrong turned his back on him and ordered Holden to take the ship out.

"Get us to Australia."

Holden ran to the wheel and followed the orders. Armstrong took one last look at the island and headed to his cabin. Once inside, he pulled out some paper and his quill. He spent the next few hours detailing what had happened. In his mind, Armstrong knew this report would convince the Queen to send ships here to harness the power of the statues.

*

"So where is this report?" Queen Victoria asked when Armstrong had finished.

"Lost at sea, Ma'am. After we delivered the prisoners and finished the business in Australia, we encountered storms that devastated the ship. Most of the hands were lost and I, Holden, and three others clung to parts of the ship until we landed on an island in the Indian Ocean. Holden and the others died, and I survived there for two years until a merchant ship visited. I had to work my passage off, and I was eventually dropped in South Africa."

"Yes, yes, I understand. You suffered for your passage home. But why do you address me in such rags?" the Queen asked.

"My wife. She declared me dead and married another man. She would have nothing to do with me when I arrived home. I decided to come here to tell my story."

"Well, it certainly is quite a story. However, before I cast judgement, let me bring in an expert."

The Queen gestured to one of her pages and soon, John Nullius walked into the room. Armstrong blinked at the sight of him.

"Mr. Nullius, I have heard an incredible story of Easter Island. Apparently, the statues move and can catch ships. Have you witnessed such event?"

Nullius regarded Armstrong, then gave him a slight smirk before answering. "Your Highness, in the eight years that I spent there cataloguing the locals, fauna, and traditions, I never saw nor heard of such an event. It's a fairy tale. The man is obviously mad."

"Nullius!" Armstrong yelled. "I visited the island. I saw you and the locals watch the statues perform that miracle!"

"Your Highness, this is the first time I have ever met this man."

Armstrong fell to his knees. The Queen motioned to the guards.

"Dungeon."

Armstrong was grabbed and dragged out of the court. In his cell later, Armstrong dreamed of the statues. He was standing on the beach, watching them rise out of the ground. He tried to run, but was grabbed and carried out to the water. The statues submerged him in the salty sea and held him there. Just as he was about to run out of air, he woke up screaming.

As he thrashed in his cell, Nullius was watching, next to one of the guards.

"That one's mad," the guard said.

Nullius said nothing. He smiled, and remembered Armstrong's revolting attitude towards both him and the islanders. He also remembered the ship that had visited the island a year after Armstrong left. Nullius had returned to England, hoping to meet Armstrong again. His wish upon the statues had been granted.

Claw

Stewart Thomas always remembered the day his brother died. It was the same day he found the ancient thing that would plague him the rest of his life.

The only picture Stewart had of his brother sat on the bedside table in his room. It portrayed two young brown-haired boys in their coveralls eating ice cream cones. Tears welled up in his eyes as he stared at the picture. Now thirty years on, Stewart could still picture the scene.

Curling, Newfoundland

Thirty years earlier

"Come on, Stewie!" Daniel yelled as he ran towards the train track. "It's coming!"

Stewart ran as fast as he could, but Daniel, being three years older, was a lot quicker. Daniel ran down the makeshift path to the tracks, which were situated behind the school they both attended. Despite continuous warnings of the dangers, kids still flocked to the tracks to stack coins on the rails. The flattened coins made for awesome souvenirs and a symbol of coolness.

Daniel was already stacking his coins when Stewart arrived. Several kids from the school out on recess had gathered at the top of the small hill to watch. As the train came around the bend, Daniel yelled to Stewart, "Come on, give me your quarters."

"No, Mom gave them to me for my milk. I want my milk, Danny."

"Crybaby," Daniel said, as he put the last of the coins on the track. As Stewart turned to head back up the hill, he noticed something strange at the edge of the track. Before he could shout a warning, Daniel stood up and tripped over the object as he tried to follow his brother.

Daniel fell onto the tracks and Stewart heard a snap. Daniel screamed in pain as he gripped his foot, which was twisted at an unnatural angle.

"Stewie, help!" Daniel cried out.

Stewart froze and couldn't move. Daniel reached out and pleaded with his brother to help him. Stewart stared, scared of the train coming towards them.

"Help him!" cried a young girl from the top of the hill. Stewart finally broke free of his fears and ran towards his brother. The train was twenty feet from them when he grabbed Daniel's hand. He pulled with all his might, but couldn't move his bigger brother. As he tried again, Stewart tripped over the strange object and fell beside the tracks.

Stewart watched in horror as the slow-moving train rolled over his brother. Daniel's screams filled his ears and etched themselves into his mind forever. The children on top of the hill screamed and ran back to the school.

Later, at the inquiry, it was found that the engineer was drunk and hadn't even noticed the boy on the tracks. Stewart, still in shock after the train had passed, glanced down to see the flattened coins and the strange object that they'd both tripped over. It was a claw.

*

Present day

Stewart stared at the small wooden box on top of the dresser in the corner of the room. It was plain, with no markings, but it contained the evil of that horrible day.

"I don't know what caused me to pick it up," Stewart had told his wife. "I mean, my brother was lying dead on the tracks, but my eyes went straight to this thing and the coins."

A picture of his wife, Susan, a blond beauty he'd met in high school, sat next to Daniel's. It was taken on a cold day on the shore of the Bay of Islands. With the famous 'Weeball' in the background, Susan smiled, her face framed by the fur of her parka.

They'd been married for ten years before she accidentally found the box in the attic of his mother's home which he'd inherited. Afterwards, the marriage soured. The evil contents filled Stewart's soul, and he pushed the only other thing he loved away. He was holding the flattened coins in his hand when the taxi carried her off.

Five years later, he still regretted the fact that he couldn't tell her why he kept the box. It was a secret. It had been several years since he'd thought about the box, and he was happy. Once the box was discovered, the reasons for its banishment to attic came back to him, and it tore his marriage apart.

Stewart glanced at the box, and memories of school came flooding back to him.

Corner Brook, Newfoundland

Twenty-seven years earlier

Stewart was slammed against the brick wall behind the school. The cause stood in front of him: Jacob Smith, school bully and all-around arsehole. Behind him stood two of his buddies with their girlfriends. Jacob's girlfriend, Denise, was egging Jacob on. They were all laughing.

"Little Stewie Tomtom. The boy who let his brother die on the tracks," Jacob said, to the delight of his little gang. "Did you cry when they threw old Danny boy in the hole?"

Stewart tried to run away, but Jacob's goons grabbed him and threw him against the wall again. Stewart's back and head were hurting. Jacob grabbed Stewart's book bag and opened it. He dumped the contents, and Stewart watched in dismay as his comics and schoolbooks fell to the ground. Jacob looked inside the bag and frowned. He reached in and pulled out an old claw.

"What the hell is this, little Stewie?"

Stewart said nothing.

"How about this? Tell me what this is, or I will turn you inside out," Jacob said, as the kids behind him laughed.

Stewart closed his eyes. He could feel the darkness fall around them. Screams and running feet filled his ears. Death filled his nose.

*

Stewart was lying on his bed in the fetal position. The horrors behind the school filled his mind as he stifled a scream. Sweat poured from his forehead and stained the pillowcase. He remembered picking up his book bag and his belongings. Then he turned and walked away from the scene.

Questions from the police followed, but he was dismissed as a suspect.

"I mean, how could a little boy possibly inflict so much damage and kill six people?" Stewart said to the box. "In the end, it was Jacob who got turned inside out."

Everyone at school treated him differently after that—not nicely but as a freak. His parents' friends started to shun them and eventually, the family moved to Ontario. Starting fresh, Stewart didn't encounter anything sinister again until high school.

*

Seventeen years earlier

St. Andrews school in St. Catharines was perfect for Stewart. Great science program, good friends, and girls. Lots of *pretty* girls. Since arriving in the Garden City, it took him a couple of years to find his place, but once he did, Stewart never looked back. He forgot about the claw, which rested in a box under his bed. He was enjoying life and, for the first time in ages, he was happy.

He was heading home after school one day when he heard muffled screams coming from an alley close to his home.

He wandered in and saw two men holding a young girl down on the ground. He recognized her as a girl from school.

One of the men turned to see Stewart. He pulled out a knife and pointed it at him. Stewart ran out of the alley as the man laughed and returned to the assault.

When he got home, Stewart went straight to his room. He dumped his books and reached under the bed, grabbing the box. He hesitated, but he felt that this was right. He opened the box and closed his eyes.

When he got back to the alley, Stewart found the girl by herself, huddled on an old piece of cardboard. There was no trace of her attackers. He helped her up and gave her some space, then introduced himself and offered to call the police. She shook her head.

They walked out of the alley and down the street before she spoke.

"Thank you. I don't think they hurt me too much."

"What happened to them?" he asked.

"I don't know. One second, they were holding me down, the next they were gone. I remember it went dark for a moment, and I was free," she paused. "My name is Susan."

*

Present day

A knock on the door brought Stewart out of his reverie. He went to the door and looked through the peephole. It was a tall, bald man wearing a black leather jacket and an Iron

Maiden t-shirt. Stewart opened the door and allowed the visitor in.

"Thank you for coming, Mr. Diggs," Stewart said. "The object is on the dresser."

Diggs went to the dresser and picked up the box. After weighing it in his hands, he turned to Stewart.

"It's amazing the amount of death that can come from such a small thing."

Stewart nodded.

"Are you sure you want to get rid of it? I mean…the power…"

"It's caused me nothing but pain. It needs to go."

Diggs pulled an envelope out of his jacket pocket and handed it to Stewart.

"As agreed, ten grand. Should help you out in the short term."

Stewart took the envelope.

"So, think your shop can hide this thing? I mean, if it gets into the wrong hands, I can't imagine the chaos and death it would bring."

Diggs turned towards the door. As he opened it, he said, "*If.*"

Stewart looked at Diggs, who was smiling.

"My shop showcases a lot of dangerous things. Voodoo, satanic books, objects for rituals, but this?" he said, patting the box. "I know a few people who would kill for this."

"It needs to be hidden," Stewart said, holding the envelope back out to Diggs. "You promised to hide it, not sell it. Just give it back."

Diggs slapped the envelope out of Stewart's hand and punched him in the stomach. Stewart fell to the floor, clutching himself. Diggs laughed.

"Sorry, Stewart. I have a lot of scores to settle, and many a person who owes me. This is the perfect tool to achieve that."

Diggs walked forward and kicked Stewart in the back, leaving him howling in pain. He went to the door, but as he began to walk out, the box pulled him back. Confused, he tried a second time. The box wouldn't leave the room.

Diggs tried a third time, only to be hauled back into the room and thrown onto the bed. The door slammed shut and the box opened. Stewart closed his eyes as the room went cold. Diggs gasped when he saw the claw float out of the box. A swirling darkness attached itself to the claw and manifested into a tall, wretched-looking creature.

Diggs screamed as the claw grabbed him and pulled him off the bed. Stewart put his hands over his ears to block out the sounds. After a minute, the screaming stopped, and the room went quiet.

Stewart opened his eyes and gingerly got to his feet. Remnants of Diggs plastered the walls, while the box lay on the bed. He gazed at the box and shook with fear.

"You didn't have to kill him," he whispered.

A knock on the door shook him back to reality. It opened; a man with a long beard and long leather coat glided into the room and handed Stewart a card. It read, 'A. Fox. Unnatural Transportation'.

"I think, Mr. Thomas, that you may need to vacate these premises," Fox said, as he looked around the room. "Take the envelope. You will need the money—and don't forget the box. You've been its guardian for many years. It's never going to let you go."

Stewart was still in shock when Fox sighed, picked up the envelope, and grabbed him by the shoulder.

"Stewart, it's time. Grab the box."

Stewart glanced at Fox and nodded. He picked up the box and allowed Fox to lead him out of the room.

"What about my arrangements? The landlord will tell the police about me."

"It's all been taken care of. Don't worry, this is what I do."

Stewart walked out of the apartment without looking back.

*

Six months later

Jack Murphy pulled himself off the cobblestones and looked down the alley. The attackers were nowhere to be seen. He hurried over to his wife, who was adjusting her skirt after the mugging and near rape. He helped her up and held her tight. She was crying.

Jack turned his head and saw blood all over the end of the alley. He also saw something that resembled human remains. As he stared at the scene, he heard a click at the mouth of the alley. He turned to see a man in a long leather coat and sunglasses. He was holding a box. The man nodded to Jack and his wife, then left.

Jack walked with his wife to the street, looking around for the stranger, but didn't see him.

Three blocks away, Stewart walked calmly, and with a sense of peace. It was like Fox said—he was the guardian of the box. As much as it cursed him, Stewart knew using it this way was better than letting it being used for evil.

The thought comforted him as he touched the box in his pocket and continued down the street.

The Wreckhouse

"If I told you once, I told you a hundred times—don't run the Wreckhouse during a storm," John's voice roared over the radio.

Tucker Wallace ignored his boss and put the hammer down, as he pushed the eighteen-wheeler through the driving wet snow. Even though the ferry had docked in Port aux Basques two hours earlier, Tucker had to pause his drive to meet his supplier, Dinkie.

"Don't delay. My man in Deer Lake is ready to run this stuff up the coast. I'm sure your boss won't quibble about you stopping for a bite to eat before the long trek to St. John's."

Tucker grunted in agreement as he took the five packages and placed them in a hidden compartment in his trailer. The lack of respect was noted by Dinkie.

"This is serious shit! Miss that rendezvous, and it will mean consequences for all of us. These aren't some outport druggies you're dealing with. These pricks are from the mainland, and they won't hesitate."

Tucker shrugged his shoulders. "My cut?"

"Upon delivery."

"Whatever." Ignoring Dinkie, Tucker climbed into the cab and fired up the engine.

Now, as he made his way up the highway, Tucker laughed.

"Old Dinkie, thinks pushing a little dope makes him an arch criminal."

Tucker, however, knew full well that the packages contained something new and more potent, and that these gangsters wouldn't give a shit about anything happening on a stormy night on the west coast of Newfoundland. Be on time or you'll be of no mind. Besides, Tucker had debts of his own to pay—the hazardous kind. This payday would clear those debts.

The howling wind brought Tucker back to the job at hand. He knew the winds at the Wreckhouse were deadly and many times he'd seen trucks overturned in the ditch. If he could get through this stretch unscathed, he could hammer down and be early for the meeting. It would be good for the delivery—and his health.

Wet snow smeared the windshield as Tucker engaged the wipers. The lack of visibility forced him to slow down. He was fifteen kilometres outside Port aux Basque when Tucker's lights spotted something reflective in the distance. He downshifted, and spotted a figure walking along the highway.

"What the hell is that idiot doing?" he wondered, slowing down. He didn't have time to pick up passengers, but something inside him told him to stop.

Tucker pulled up next to the figure and engaged the brakes. He felt the cab shift as the person climbed up and opened the door. A young elfin face stared at him from under her parka hood. Tucker smiled.

"Need a lift?"

The young woman climbed into the cab and shut the door. Tucker engaged the interior lights as his new passenger pulled her hood back. Long blond hair fell over the young girl's shoulders as she unzipped her coat.

"Put your coat back here," Tucker said. pointing to his sleeper. The girl casually threw her coat on the small bed and straightened herself out.

"Two questions. Who and where?" Tucker asked.

The girl answered, "Sally Mcgee. St. John's."

Tucker studied Sally. It was a long journey to the provincial capital; he would work on her. He envisioned them sharing his bed. He smiled at the nasty things he would do to her.

"Alright, but I need to stop in Deer Lake. Have some business. Shouldn't take too long. Hope you don't mind."

"No matter to me," Sally answered.

Tucker grunted and disengaged the interior lights. He put the truck in gear and slowly pulled ahead. Tucker glanced at the girl again, feeding his desires. He was also struck by the name. It was familiar to him; however, he couldn't place it. He pushed the thought away and concentrated on the road.

After a few minutes of silence, Sally asked, "You're not going to ask me where I'm from?"

Tucker snorted. "Does it matter?"

"I guess not," Sally answered. "How about what I was doing out on the highway at this time of night."

"Lady, at this point, I need to concentrate on the road. I have deadlines to make. So sorry if I'm not really giving a shit about who you are right now."

"Fair enough," Sally said, stretching out her arms above her head. Tucker glanced out of the corner of his eye. Sally was small, but nice and fit. Her black turtleneck hugged her body, and he envisioned ripping off her jeans. He shook his head and turned his attention to the road.

"This is some truck," Sally said. "When I saw you coming up the road, you looked like an Angler fish coming out of the darkness."

"A what?" Tucker asked.

"You remember, that monster fish from *Finding Nemo*? Real nightmare fuel. I felt like a small fish about to be eaten."

Tucker smiled at the analogy. He hoped in a few hours it would be true. He stared out the window at the blackness of the night. The silence in the cab was deafening. He could hear her breathing, and it made his pulse race. He took a couple of deep breaths to get it under control.

As they passed the sign for Codroy Valley, Sally piped up. "Soon be at the Wreckhouse, eh?"

Tucker grunted. "I know all about the Wreckhouse."

"Strong winds. Betcha they're wicked out there tonight."

"Possibly."

"Did you know that when the trains used to run on the Rock, the winds were strong enough to knock the trains off the track."

"So?"

"In fact, the Railway once ignored the gentleman who used to provide the wind gust info. Twenty-two cars derailed. Bad scene."

Tucker said nothing.

"Lockie MacDougall, that was his name. Had a way with the land, Ol' Lockie did. Could tell the strength of the wind just by standing out in it. He and his wife Emily lived in the Wreckhouse. Tough Newfoundlanders they were."

"Is that a fact," Tucker said.

"True as true can be," Sally stretched out again. "They also say that you can see the ghost train run through the Wreckhouse on a stormy night, waiting for souls."

Tucker snorted and downshifted as they came over a small rise. He could already feel the wind shaking the truck. For the first time on this trip, Tucker started to question his decision to run through the area. His thoughts went to the five packages, and Dinkie's threats.

"What kind of business do you have in Deer Lake?" Sally asked.

"The 'none of your business' kind," Tucker replied.

"Rude," Sally said. "Does it have anything to do with those five packages in the trailer?"

Tucker shot her a look and returned to the road. "What five packages?" he asked, brushing off her question.

"The five that old Dinkie 'The Rat' Robinson gave you," Sally stated. "Everyone knows you run drugs for him."

Tucker concentrated on the road, but inside he was seething. How did this stupid girl know about the dope? Goddamn Dinkie. He was always running his mouth after a few pints. Small town gossip—easy to point the finger at a fucking low life with money and no job.

"Old Tucker the Trucker, they call you," Sally continued. "Dinkie's bitch. He's the dealer and you're the wheeler. Why should he get his hands dirty when you can take the rap for him."

Tucker's knuckles were turning white as he gripped the wheel. Evil thoughts entered his mind.

"Oh, I know those thoughts. What are you thinking about, Ol' Tucker? How to get rid of me or silence me? That would crush those dreams about sleeping with me."

Tucker turned to Sally, who was smiling at him. Before he could say anything, Sally piped up and pointed ahead of them.

"There's the sign."

Tucker looked back at the road and saw the fortified wooden sign for the Wreckhouse. Even half-covered in snow, Tucker could still make out the train engine portrayed above the lettering. The whole area opened in front of them.

"Oh, the wind's blowing hard out there," Sally said. "Even Ol' Lockie wouldn't be out on a night like this."

Tucker felt the whole cab rattle as he entered the open area. He could feel the trailer swinging behind him. He downshifted, which steadied it.

"Are you're sure you don't know my name?" Sally asked. Tucker downshifted again. He didn't dare touch the brakes with all the snow on the roads. He shook his head.

"Are you sure? It happened around here somewhere. Sean Blake was his name. Did awful things to me. He rides the train now."

"What bloody train are you talking about?" Tucker yelled as he fought for control of the truck. "There hasn't a fucking train here in years."

"That one." Sally pointed out the passenger window.

Tucker turned his gaze towards where Sally was pointing, then stared in horror as a silvery white train emerged out of the snow and ran along the side of the highway. He could see into the windows of the cars. Ghostly figures, with deep black holes instead of eyes, were pointing at him. Tucker could hear a low humming coming over his radio. It sounded like chanting. Tucker soon realized the chant was his name.

"Tuck-er. Tuck-er. Tuck-er," Sally chanted along with the radio.

Tucker let the wheel slip through his fingers. He could see the figures reaching out through the windows. He turned back to the road and screamed as he saw several ghostly figures on the road in front of him.

Panicking, Tucker hit the brakes. The truck swerved to the left. As Tucker tried to respond, he saw the trailer jackknifing in the side mirror. He had seconds before the trailer smashed into the side of the truck. The side window exploded, pelting Tucker's face with broken glass.

"Whee!" Sally yelled.

Tucker, stunned from the impact, lost control of the wheel. The truck straightened out, and the front wheels caught the side of the ditch. Tucker's world went upside down as the truck flipped over. The force of the impact wrenched the trailer free, and it fell on its side.

Chaos reigned inside the cab. Papers and food wrappers flew around the cab, and time seemed to slow for Tucker as he saw Sally floating in the air. Then he hit the roof of the cab.

The truck landed upside down. Tucker groaned from the pain in his legs. Reaching up and grabbing the wheel, Tucker pulled himself up into a sitting position. Stars filled his eyes as he glanced down at his legs, then threw up. The shin bones were sticking out through his pant legs. He realized that he was alone in the cab.

Through the broken windshield, he saw the glow of the train, which had stopped. Several ghostly figures walked towards the truck. He recognized Sally. She stepped through the walls of the cab and stood in front of Tucker.

"Ah, Mr. Wallace, it seems you're in a bit of a jam. Don't worry though, because you will soon be on the train. It has a special car that's just for people like you."

Tucker groaned and nodded. He lay back and felt his life leave him.

"I wouldn't worry about being alone for long, though. From what I understand, Dinkie will be joining the train in a few days. All over a few packages of self-destruction."

Tucker closed his eyes. When he opened them again, he was on the train. He saw Sally waving at him as the train pulled away. It would be the last moment of peace he would ever have.

Acknowledgments

There are many people to thank when a book gets published. Suzanne Craig-Whytock at DarkWinter Press and Literary Magazine, who saw the potential and published many of my short stories before my first book. Cheers to you and many heartfelt thanks.

My family and friends whose kind words and encouragement kept me going.

My friends in our Niagara Writers group, whose critiques and excellent advice kept pushing me to get better. Oh yeah, get your submissions in for the next meeting.

Finally, and most importantly, my wife Angela and our daughter Kate. Cheers to you both for all your love and support. I couldn't do it without you.

About The Author

Originally from Corner Brook, Newfoundland and Labrador, Christopher Butt is a twenty-year veteran of the Canadian Military. He is also the author of several published short stories and a collection, *In the Lair of the Kraken* (DarkWinter Press). He currently lives in St. Catharines, Ontario.